TimeOut50

TimeOut50

50 YEARS, 50 COVERS

Edited by James Manning
Design by Tom Hislop

Editor-in-chief: Caroline McGinn

UNICORN

First published in 2018 by Unicorn
an imprint of Unicorn Publishing Group LLP
5 Newburgh Street
London W1F 7RG
www.unicornpublishing.org

Every effort has been made to trace copyright
holders and to obtain their permission for the use of
copyright material. The publisher apologises for
any errors or omissions in the list below or credits
throughout and would be grateful if notified (via
email to hello@timeout.com) of any corrections that
should be incorporated in future reprints or editions
of this book.

Text © Time Out Group, 2018.
Introduction adapted from the Somerset House
podcast 'Print | Tony Elliott' by Eleanor Scott, with
additional interview material by James Manning.
Captions by Tristan Parker, Sonya Barber, Laura Lee
Davies, James Manning, Megan Carnegie, Rose
Johnstone, Chris Waywell and Liz Tray.
Picture research by Ben Rowe. Images: p8 photo
Andy Parsons; p9 photo Don Morley © Guardian
News & Media Ltd 2018; p39 photo David James
© 1976 Studiocanal Films Ltd. All rights reserved;
p51 www.redsaundersphoto.eu; p93 Courtesy
Pest Control Office; p101 © Tracey Emin. All rights
reserved, DACS 2018; p127 Kate Booker.
10 9 8 7 6 5 4 3 2 1
ISBN 978-1-911604-9-14
Printed in Spain by GraphyCems

www.timeout.com

Contents

Foreword

Tony Elliott, founder

"I started Time Out in 1968 when I was a 21-year-old student at Keele University. I was always interested in new, radical things in theatre, art, film and music. What's now called the counterculture was in full flight, but it was hard to decide what you were going to go and see: the information was in lots of different places, and in some cases not very well done. There used to be a magazine called *What's On*, which was very straight and rather dull. My plan was to do a hip *What's On*. So effectively I created a publication for myself – and, as it turned out, a lot of other people got it immediately.

The first issue was pocket-sized: the equivalent of eight pages of what we do today. An eclectic range of subjects was covered: music, theatre, film, food, art, architecture… Time Out was a kind of survival guide to getting the best out of living in London, as well as a reflection of what was happening. We always supported new and up-and-coming culture: things that were pushing back against the established infrastructure, while adding to it at the same time. We still do that to this day.

The first few years of establishing the project were thrilling. Time Out initially came out every three weeks, and there was literally just me and a couple of other people. We had no money: we were funding it out of the income from issue to issue. But I was constantly exploring how to make things bigger and better. We became fortnightly within a year, and in April 1971 we went weekly. Circulation and advertising were building, which meant that we could produce ever bigger magazines. Things gradually expanded. Theatre and other sections started to include comprehensive listings.

In the early '70s, there were quite a lot of political publications – *Black Dwarf*, *Red Mole*, *Spare Rib* – but there weren't that many strong, wide-ranging cultural publications. We were a bright light, I suppose: the one magazine that covered the new underground, independent culture alongside the best of the mainstream. But we were not really part of the "underground press". Time Out was considered quite straight. We wanted a publication that was well designed, well put together and efficient. It was all about the information – and in many ways, it still is.

People often talk about Time Out, in its early years, being political. Yes, we were political, but with a small "p". We were running information from a political environment. We did a lot of coverage of the Troubles in Northern Ireland, and about the Metropolitan Police and the way that they behaved towards groups such as squatters and black people. What we published was a package: it wasn't just arts and culture and it wasn't just politics, and that was one of the reasons people responded so well to it. Well, most people. Mick Jagger once told one editor: "The problem with Time Out is that you have to cross a picket line to get to the music listings."

We had a fantastic designer who worked with Time Out in the early '70s and then carried on doing covers on a freelance basis, called Pearce Marchbank. We made a huge effort to have great covers, and in the early days – when we had a sort of monopoly, because nobody else was doing what we were doing – we could take enormous risks. There was no circulation department standing over the designers, so we could run covers that were just one word, like Pearce's fantastic "Jealousy" cover (p29).

Pearce also kept the typography very recognisable. To this day, people can pick up a Time Out product anywhere in the world and they know it's ours because of the Franklin Gothic typeface.

'We made a huge effort to have great covers'

Time Out has been published in London every week for 47 years with just one interruption. At one point, a negotiation with unionised staff resulted in most people at Time Out being paid the same amount. After a few years, we decided that it was the right thing to do to introduce a more conventional pay scale. In 1981, the stand-off came to its inevitable conclusion: a long strike. Forty-two people quit to go and start up a rival publication, *City Limits*. The readership also split.

When Time Out returned to print after four long months, I was able to re-evaluate a lot of things in the magazine: introducing a nightlife and clubs section, for one thing. We wanted to reflect the fact that the spectrum of London life had evolved.

By the late '80s, we had a solid base in London and I started thinking of setting up magazines in other cities. Most UK cities outside London weren't big enough to support the kind of infrastructure that you need to do something like Time Out, so we looked abroad. Some early experiments in various European cities – Paris, Amsterdam and Berlin – weren't successful in the long run, but we had established the first international links.

I'd had a burning desire to do Time Out in New York

↑
A Time Out editorial meeting in 1972. From left to right: news editor David May, Tony Elliott, music editor John Fordham and advertising director John Leaver

←
Tony Elliott in July 2018, photographed by Andy Parsons

ever since I first visited the city in 1973. In 1992, after we'd reached a degree of financial stability in London, I finally went to New York to start looking for investors. We launched Time Out New York in 1995, which was largely an overnight success. It proved that the brand could travel.

We then got a steady trickle of people coming to us from other places, starting with Istanbul, then Dubai, Russia, Israel, China and Australia – all wanting to do Time Out in their own cities. So we developed a licensing system. We knew that, sitting in London, we shouldn't think that we can just arrive in a foreign city and get it right, so we've always worked with local experts. Today Time Out has a presence in 108 cities across the world.

In the mid-'90s, the internet came along and you could put any question into a search engine and get an answer. But online and digital never held any fears for me. Time Out is the perfect thing for online, because that's an ideal environment for making our data available: not just the name of an event, where it's on and when, but also what I call "the information about the information": the critical viewpoint.

We are 100 percent committed to digital: it's what we do. But we keep a physical printed form

where it's appropriate and financially viable. In London, we had to go from publishing a big, paid-for magazine to a free one. The paid circulation was declining, and there was a critical point looming where the sales would go below, say, 50,000 copies a week, which would mean we lost significance for advertisers. So in 2012 we decided to go free, and suddenly we were putting out 300,000 copies with a multiple readership: up to 600,000 or 700,000 readers in total.

And one of the great things that happened there – which wasn't foreseen, if I'm honest – was that hundreds of thousands of young readers entered our world. Up to that point, they'd felt excluded because of the cover price and the daunting size of the magazine. But that younger, more digital audience really responded to the free magazine, discovering the Time Out brand for the first time and going on to use timeout.com and the Time Out app. It was a big success, which we've replicated elsewhere.

It's easier now than it's ever been before to tell people about something exciting. But our mission is the same as it was in 1968: to be the definitive, go-to portal for information on the very best of the city.'

London, 2018

The Time Out story

1983
Time Out goes to court and launches a campaign to fight for its right to publish TV listings. Richard Branson's Time Out rival *Event* fails to stay afloat.

1982
Don Atyeo and Jerome Burne become co-editors. Time Out runs its first full-colour feature. Comprehensive TV listings are published for the first time, following the launch of Channel 4, and immediately injuncted by copyright holders.

1981
A unionised staff strike halts production of Time Out for four months. Forty-two members of staff leave and set up rival publication *City Limits*. Time Out returns in September with Tony Elliott as editor.

1980
Police marksmen raid the Time Out offices, after staffers take to the roof for a photoshoot with balaclavas and replica guns.

1979
Time Out covers the Northern Irish conflict and 'Alien'. Barry Miles spends six months as editor.

1984
Time Out publishes its first 'Eating & Drinking Guide' to London and scores an exclusive interview with Al Pacino.

1985
Jerome Burne leaves; Don Atyeo remains as editor. Time Out buys a 50 percent stake in style bible *i-D* magazine.

1986
George Michael sues the magazine for reneging on a promise to put him on the cover.

1988
Simon Garfield becomes Time Out editor. Clubs editor Dave Swindells goes on an acid house bender in the name of research. Time Out acquires *Paris Passion* magazine.

1989
Time Out launches a national arts magazine, *20/20*, which folds after 16 months. A London city guide book is more successful; the new range eventually covers more than 40 cities.

2010
Oakley Capital invests in Time Out to clear its debts and provide working capital for expansion and future growth. Time Out launches its e-commerce platform.

2009
Time Out London appoints Mark Frith as editor and launches an iPhone app.

2007
'The hipster must die!' declares the cover of Time Out New York.

2004
Gordon Thomson takes the London editor's seat. Time Out New York launches a successful Kids magazine.

2002
The Time Out logo gains a red city bar: its first change since 1986. Time Out launches an online dating service.

2011
Former comedy editor Tim Arthur takes over as editor of the London magazine.

2012
Daniel Radcliffe guest edits Time Out London. In September, the magazine switches to free distribution, boosting circulation from 52,198 to 305,530.

2013
Caroline McGinn becomes editor of Time Out London – now the city's most widely read free magazine. Time Out Group starts bringing franchises in-house, starting with Chicago.

2014
The first Time Out Market brings the best of Lisbon under one roof. Time Out London moves office to Shaftesbury Avenue and launches the first Love City Awards, with readers nominating their favourite local spots.

2015
Julio Bruno joins Time Out as executive chairman. Time Out New York follows London to the brave new world of free distribution. Time Out Portugal comes in-house: *bem-vindos!*

1968
Tony Elliott launches Time Out magazine in London.

1969
Time Out goes fortnightly, circulation reaches 10,000 and the first section editors join. Marc Bolan drops by to take out a full-page advert for his book of poetry.

1970
Time Out moves from its basement offices on Princedale Road to 374 Gray's Inn Road. Jeremy Beadle launches a short-lived Time Out spin-off in the north-west of England.

1971
Time Out changes size and goes weekly. The first Time Out guidebook, 'The Book of London', is published.

1972
Tony Elliott hands over the editorship of Time Out to John Lloyd. Circulation reaches 30,000.

1978
John Fordham becomes editor. Time Out supports the Rock Against Racism campaign.

1977
Writers Duncan Campbell and Crispin Aubrey are arrested by Special Branch officers after interviewing a GCHQ whistleblower. Time Out moves to Tower House on Southampton Street.

1976
Time Out publishes 'Red Pages', a directory of radical community organisations in London, but mostly fails to cover the exploding punk scene. Richard Williams becomes editor.

1975
Time Out launches a consumer magazine, 'Sell Out', with Janet Street-Porter as editor.

1973
David May and Jerome Burne become co-editors. Time Out launches an annual 'Student Guide'.

1990
Time Out interviews an unknown artist named Damien Hirst. John Morrish becomes editor. City guides to Paris and New York appear.

1991
TV listings are deregulated and Time Out introduces a comprehensive TV and radio guide. The first 'Time Out Film Guide' is published.

1992
Dominic Wells takes over as editor. Cover stars include Madonna and Macaulay Culkin.

1993
Time Out moves to 251 Tottenham Court Road and experiments with a monthly magazine in Amsterdam.

1995
Time Out New York becomes the brand's first weekly magazine outside the UK. Time Out London's circulation peaks at 110,496. Meanwhile, the first Time Out website launches.

2001
Time Out Istanbul launches as the first international franchisee, swiftly followed by Time Out Dubai. World domination beckons.

1999
Vicky Mayer becomes London editor for just six months. Julian Rhind-Tutt plays a Time Out writer in Richard Curtis's film 'Notting Hill'.

1998
Laura Lee Davies becomes Time Out London's first female editor. Time Out celebrates 30 years with a party at Brixton Academy.

1997
Time Out London sponsors the controversial 'Sensation' exhibition of Young British Artists.

1996
Time Out interviews an unknown pop group called the Spice Girls and launches an 'Eating & Drinking Guide' to Paris.

2016
Time Out Group plc launches on the AIM stock exchange. Time Out New York moves to 1540 Broadway. Free magazines launch in Los Angeles and Miami.

2017
Time Out London moves to 77 Wicklow Street with Gail Tolley as editor. Tony Elliott receives a CBE for services to publishing and an Outstanding Contribution to British Media award. Franchises in Australia, Spain, Singapore and Hong Kong become part of Time Out Group.

2018
Time Out celebrates its fiftieth birthday, launches free magazines in Paris, Madrid and Hong Kong and wins PPA's 'International Media Brand of the Year' award for the fifth time in nine years. Now, what's next?

TIME OUT
London
Aug 12-Sept 2

1s

The first issue of Time Out was printed on an A2 sheet and folded down to A5. With listings for 'Buildings', 'Blueish Films', and 'Rabbit Food' as well as art, music and theatre, it was a snapshot of London culture at the time. Tony Elliott cut out the cover image from a publicity shot for the 'Cybernetic Serendipity' exhibition at the new Institute of Contemporary Arts. 'It didn't stereotype Time Out as a hip music or fashion magazine,' Elliott explains. 'It felt completely right.'

01

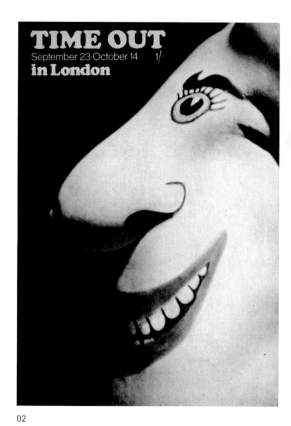

02

01 **September 1968**
Photography
Ray Stevenson

02 **September 1968**
Body painting
Alan Aldridge

03 **November 1968**

04 **January 1969**

03

04

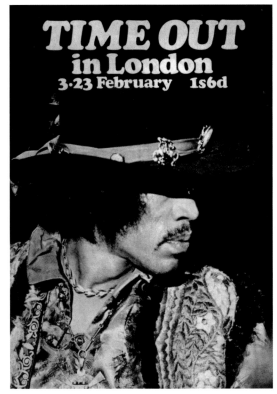

05

06

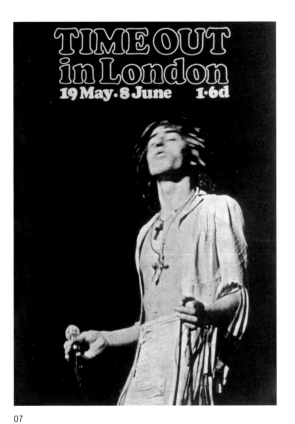

07

08

05 **February 1969**

06 **April 1969**

07 **May 1969**
Photography
Eric Hayes

08 **August 1969**
Illustration
Michael English

'Fifty-three years ago. a number of us tried to start a London "listings magazine" called *London Life*... and failed. Three years later, Tony Elliott did the same and succeeded – brilliantly. Congratulations!'

Lord Puttnam, film producer

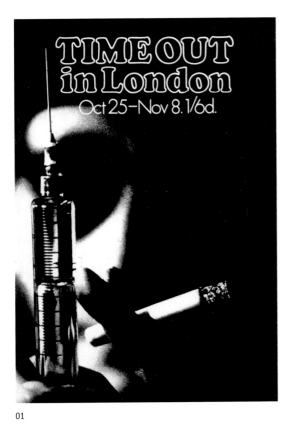

01

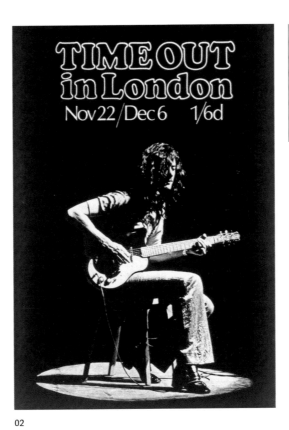

02

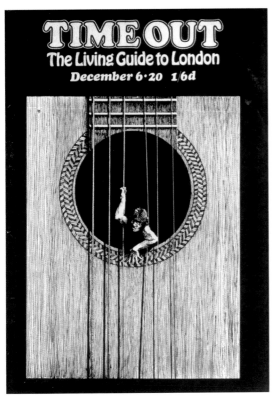

03

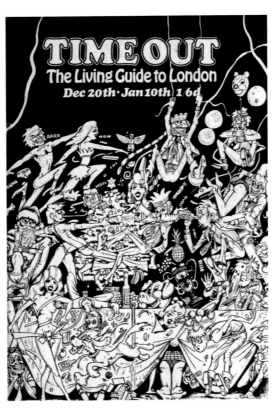

04

Time Out

The Living Guide to London
March 7 -21
15p 3/-

Warhol's

EXCLUSIVE

TIME OUT INTERVIEW

Inside Time Out

Just three years after its inception, Time Out scored an exclusive interview with Andy Warhol when he opened his show at the Tate Gallery. The Warhol-pastiche cover was by versatile illustrator Peter Brookes, later one of Britain's leading political cartoonists. 'I used to call him "Dial-a-Style",' says designer Pearce Marchbank, 'because he could do you a Hogarth today and a Renoir tomorrow.'

Pearce Marchbank

Design director and consultant 1970-83

'When Time Out went weekly, it was an opportunity to clean the whole thing up. I shaped it into the sections which are still basically extant, and brought in a news section. Before that, there had been no journalism at all in the magazine.

My great guru for cover design is George Lois, who worked on *Esquire* magazine in the '60s and '70s. He was an advertising man, and he put one major idea on the front cover which grabbed people. You've got about three seconds of the punter's time looking at a magazine cover, so you need an image that you can see over the street. Anyone who has the guts to do a cover that's all one colour or a very simple image will turn all the opposition on the newsstand into background noise.

The logo was supposed to be temporary: I had to knock it up one Sunday afternoon. The idea was that the logo would be like writing on a window.

That's why it wasn't solid lettering: it was hovering on the surface of the cover and you'd see through it to the main cover image. If you look through the early weekly covers, we often obscured the logo almost to the point of illegibility, but people knew perfectly well what it was.

I introduced Franklin Gothic to Time Out because it's a typeface that can work with any subject. It's the voice of the magazine: a voice that can say anything. It also had a certain personality: it wasn't cold like Helvetica. It never goes out of date because it was never fashionable.

The budgets were minimal and the deadlines were tight. I had about two days from the original discussion with the editors to the delivery of artwork, so often we worked through the night. Looking back at the covers, it's amazing we managed to do it.'

David May

Co-editor 1973-75

'The early-to-mid-'70s have a grey reputation, but we had free festivals, great rock bands, Bowie as Ziggy and punk just coming over the horizon, as well as agitprop and political demos. We were young, energetic, and deeply involved in London's counterculture – and we threw great parties.

I was the only traditionally trained journalist on the magazine when I joined as the first news editor. Our journalistic and critical freedom flowed from our economic and editorial independence. We were in the forefront covering civil liberties, gay and women's rights, the homeless, benefit claimants and black and immigrant communities. We exposed police and political corruption, uncovered secret service "dirty tricks",

investigated drugs issues and campaigned against the destruction of historic areas of London like Covent Garden. My co-editor Jerome Burne and I more than doubled the circulation, but we also faced intense police pressure, legal threats, Special Branch visits and cautions – followed by my arrest and Old Bailey trial.

As the design director, Pearce Marchbank gave the magazine its logo, its look and its editorial structure. He always did the unexpected with covers. If every other title had the same interview, show, exhibition or celebrity, Pearce would do something different. He was John Lennon to Tony Elliott's Paul McCartney, and together they created a groundbreaking magazine.'

Richard Williams

Editor 1976-78

'We were at the centre of a city full of new things, to which we had privileged access. There wasn't anything else remotely like Time Out in London at the time. Everything in the magazine was filtered through the attitude of the counterculture – not just the news and the features, but the coverage of the arts and even sport. In 1977, I introduced a disco column and the staff (who were almost entirely committed to pub rock) hated it. There might even have been a little strike. The office was lively, disputatious, political (with a large and small 'p') and very committed. I remember our production editor, a large bluff Lancastrian, coming to work with a lapel badge bearing the message: "How dare you assume I'm heterosexual?" And I may have chaired the first editorial conference at a London publication to feature a breastfeeding theatre editor.'

John Fordham

Editor 1978-79 and 1979-81

'Time Out had no serious rivals in the 1970s. *What's On* (known by the Time Out staff as *What's Off*) had become a bland publication aimed at tourists, and no other press were interested in such comprehensive detail about what was going on in London. In Time Out, you'd get fringe and experimental stuff covered that hardly anybody else was noticing, and a different critical angle because of the radical politics of many of the writers. It's hard to overestimate how big an influence Time Out had. It made most other sources of information about London life look dated, and many of our news stories led to real changes.

Pearce Marchbank worked from his own studio, hated meetings, and liked making decisions fast, so we always worked out cover copy over the phone. His covers meant that Time Out would always jump out from the competition on the newsstand.'

'The arrival of Time Out in 1968 transformed my life and the ability of small cinemas, galleries and theatres to attract an audience. All kinds of small-scale arts venture suddenly became viable thanks to a simple idea carried through with determination and style.'

Nicholas Serota, chair of Arts Council England

→
December 1971
Illustration
Peter Brookes
Design
Pearce Marchbank

In the 1970s, beyond the dedicated music papers, there weren't that many outlets that championed popular music alongside other art forms. Time Out was one of them, and for this cover, illustrator Peter Brookes set out to recreate Frank Zappa's iconic face as a musical score, elevating the rock musician to the status of classical composer. 'If it turned out resembling the complicated jumble Zappa might have written,' Brookes says, 'so much the better.'

Time Out

The Living Guide To All London's Events December 17-23 10p
Zappa Scores 200

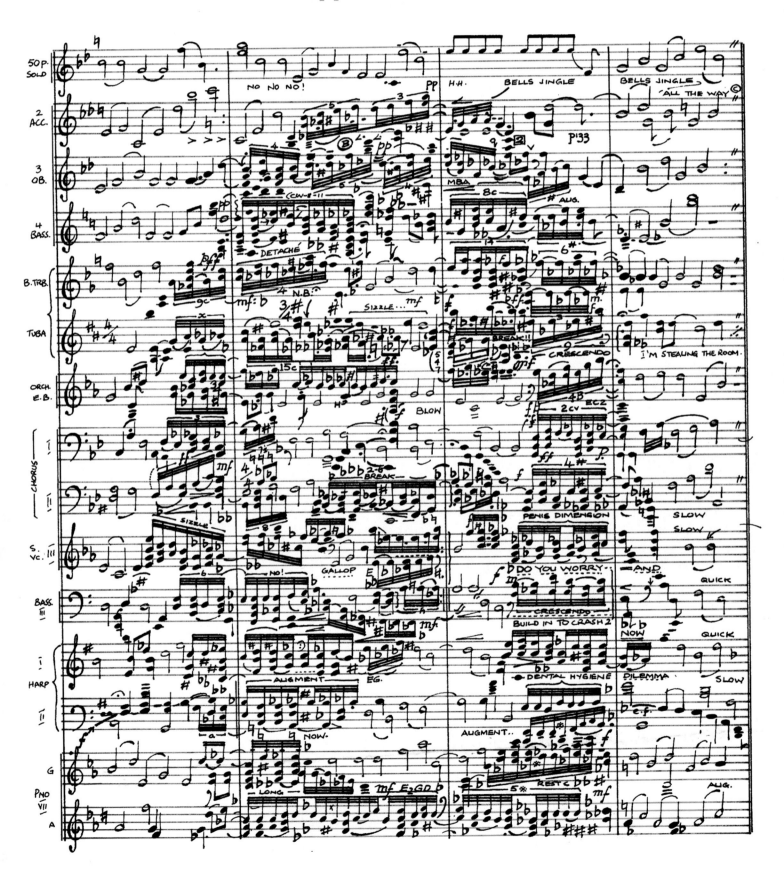

01

02

03

04

→

July 1971
Design
Pearce Marchbank
Illustration
Peter Brookes

Ever since since an 'all-night London' supplement in 1969, nocturnal city life has been a perennial Time Out theme. This is the first in a long line of 'all-night' covers, with the illustrated neon-style lettering mirroring the half-tone Time Out logo introduced in 1970. Meant as a stopgap, the logo has lasted for 48 years with only minor tweaks.

01 **September 1981**
Design
Howard Brown

02 **November 2000**
Photography
Tony Gibson

03 **March 2016**
Photography
Rob Greig
Artwork
Justin Metz
Neon
God's Own Junkyard

04 **December 1987**
Design
Simon Gunn and
Amanda Wood
Illustration
Mikki Rain
Special effects photography
Chris Booth

Time Out

**The complete guide
to all events in London
July 9-15 10p**

All-
Night
Lond n

'Suddenly, there was Time Out: just what we needed. In no time it had become an integral part of our lives. It was glorious.'

Mike Leigh, film and theatre writer-director

→
May 1973
Design
Monty Python

In 1973, Time Out had its first and most surreal guest editors: legendary British comic troupe Monty Python. Spoof adverts and listings injected the group's irreverent humour throughout the whole magazine. The cover features the distinctive, anarchic cut-out visuals of Python animator and member Terry Gilliam.

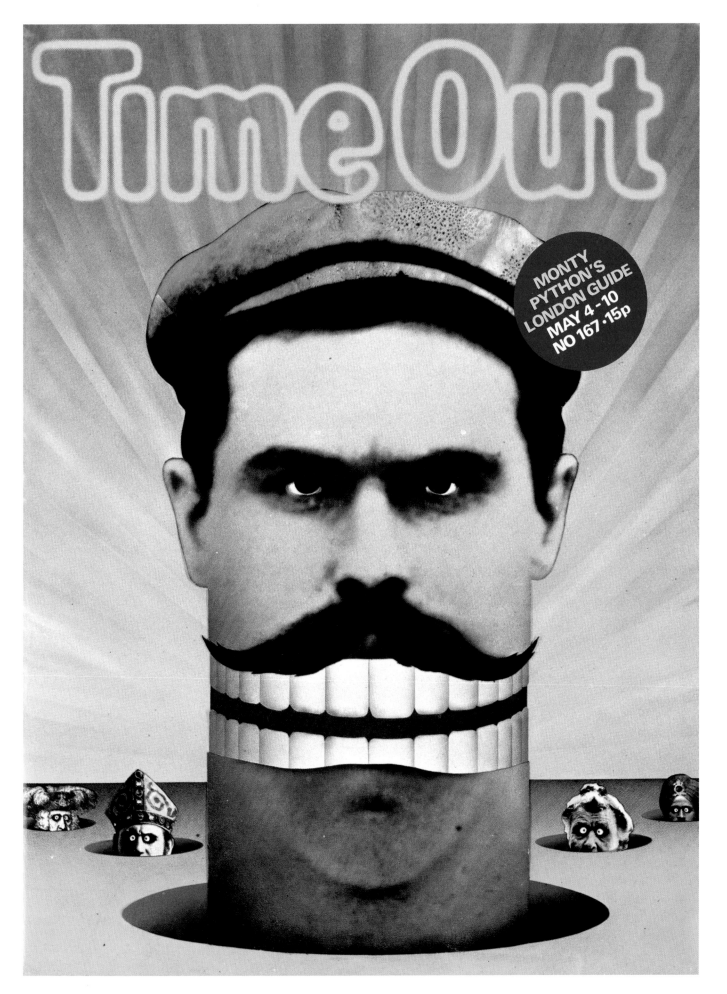

'I don't know how you could function in London without Time Out. All the nitty-gritty news and write-ups on the happenings all over town!'

Barbara Hulanicki, fashion designer and founder of Biba

→
October 1973
Design
Pearce Marchbank

When Time Out ran a piece by feminist writer Karen Durbin on how sexual jealousy was becoming a sin in the liberated age, designer Pearce Marchbank decided that just one word, set on the colour of envy, would get the job done. 'I won a fantastic battle with the money people in Time Out about the "Jealousy" cover because it sold out immediately,' Marchbank has said. 'It was before the days when people thought you had to put the whole contents of the magazine on the cover.'

Time Out

October 12-18 1973 No.190 15p

Jealousy

You're liberated.
You're hip.
You don't mind.
Do you?

→
November 1974
Design
Pearce Marchbank
Photography
Roger Perry

As Britain's press went into sycophantic overload to mark Sir Winston Churchill's hundredth anniversary, Time Out took a very different view. Marchbank and regular Time Out photographer Roger Perry subverted Churchill's famous V-sign to express an iconoclastic, alternative take on the old imperialist's legacy, with the cleaner in their shared Clerkenwell studio literally lending a hand.

'In 1968 I was working at Cramer Saatchi. We'd created a campaign to launch Island Records' new bands, written by respected music critics rather than record execs. We'd met Tony Elliott, with his passion for this new listings magazine that wasn't going to be dry and dull. This, we thought, was the perfect media for our challenging, daring campaign. The rest is history.'

Sir John Hegarty, advertising executive

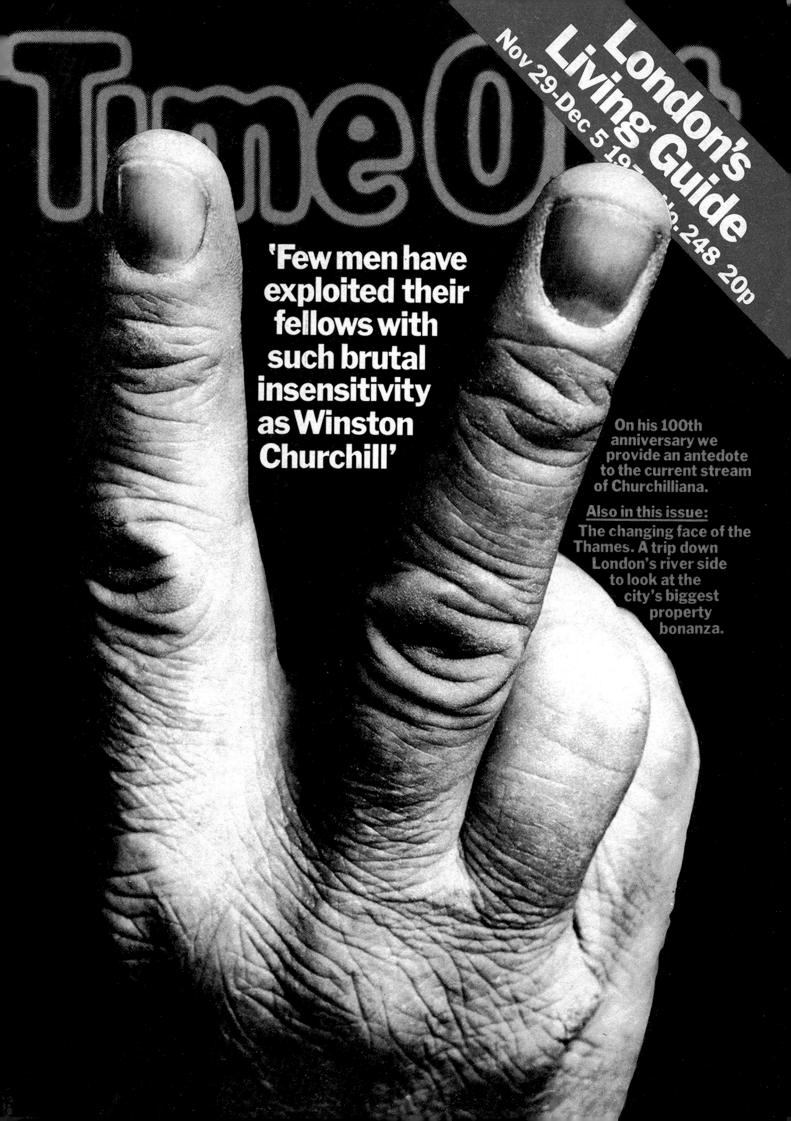

Time Out

London's
Living Guide
Nov 29-Dec 5 19   No. 248 20p

'Few men have
exploited their
fellows with
such brutal
insensitivity
as Winston
Churchill'

On his 100th
anniversary we
provide an antedote
to the current stream
of Churchilliana.

Also in this issue:
The changing face of the
Thames. A trip down
London's river side
to look at the
city's biggest
property
bonanza.

'In the mid-to-late 1970s, Time Out was staffed by an incompatible bunch of dogged leftists and a generally apolitical cadre of internationalist aesthetes. The two groupings were mutually mistrustful but mostly pretty amiable.'

Jonathan Meades, writer, filmmaker and Time Out contributor

→
October 1974
Design
Pearce Marchbank
Illustration
Trevor Sutton

Among the many causes Time Out championed in the '70s was the opposition to the 'modernisation' of chunks of London – represented here by a Godzilla-style tower block monster. 'I always worked closely with the editors so that the picture and headline on the cover should work together exactly,' remembers Pearce Marchbank. 'Trevor Sutton was extremely clever at photomontages, doing things that you can do instantly in Photoshop now, but which were then very complicated.'

Time Out

London's Living Guide
October 4-10 1974 No. 240 20p

Planners On The Rampage

The shape of our cities and the style of our lives are powerfully influenced by the planners. Who are they? What are their real objectives and how can they be influenced themselves?

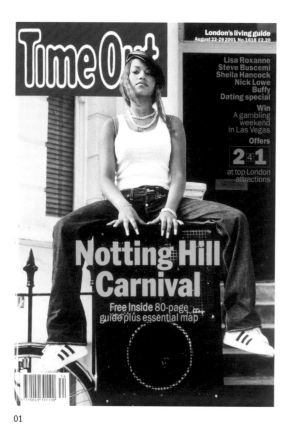

01

02

03

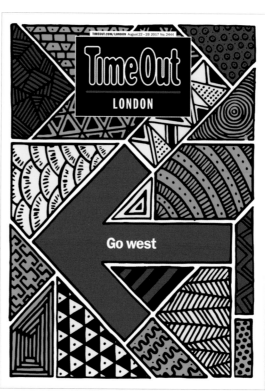

04

→

August 1975

Photography
Angela Phillips

As Notting Hill Carnival marked its tenth birthday, the city's biggest street party faced criticism over how it was organised – a debate that still rages. For the first of many Carnival covers, Time Out traced the origins of the 'Mas' (from the word 'masquerade') in Ladbroke Grove, and talked to its passionate supporters. Carnival attendance that year jumped from 100,000 to 250,000.

01 **August 2001**
Styling
Cynthia Lawrence

02 **August 1999**
Photography
Tony Gibson

03 **August 1990**
Design
Gerry Sandford
Photography
Martin Evening
Model
Angie, B/2 Agency

04 **August 2017**
Illustration
Tom Havell

Time Out

London's Living Guide

August 22-28 1975 No.284 20p

The Mas in the Grove

Notting Hill throbs with drums and street dancing for the tenth holiday Carnival.

'I am a Londoner through and through. Although I know my version of London, over the years I've needed Time Out to show me all the things I hadn't discovered, from clubs and small cinemas to the specialist shops, unique galleries and one-off happenings which make this the most exciting city in the world. Time Out made London accessible to everyone.'

Janet Street-Porter, journalist, broadcaster and former Time Out editor

→
February 1975
Design
Pearce Marchbank
Photography
Roger Perry

Why did a magazine about living in London feature a pair of feet ready to push up the daisies on its cover? In the 1970s, cultural publishing had a completely open brief. Chris Langham's feature had started life as a potentially amusing account of what happens in London when you die, but turned into an essay on how we still live with fearful Victorian attitudes to pegging out. The eye-catching cover featured a photograph by Roger Perry of his girlfriend's feet, and designer Pearce Marchbank's real-life address on the label.

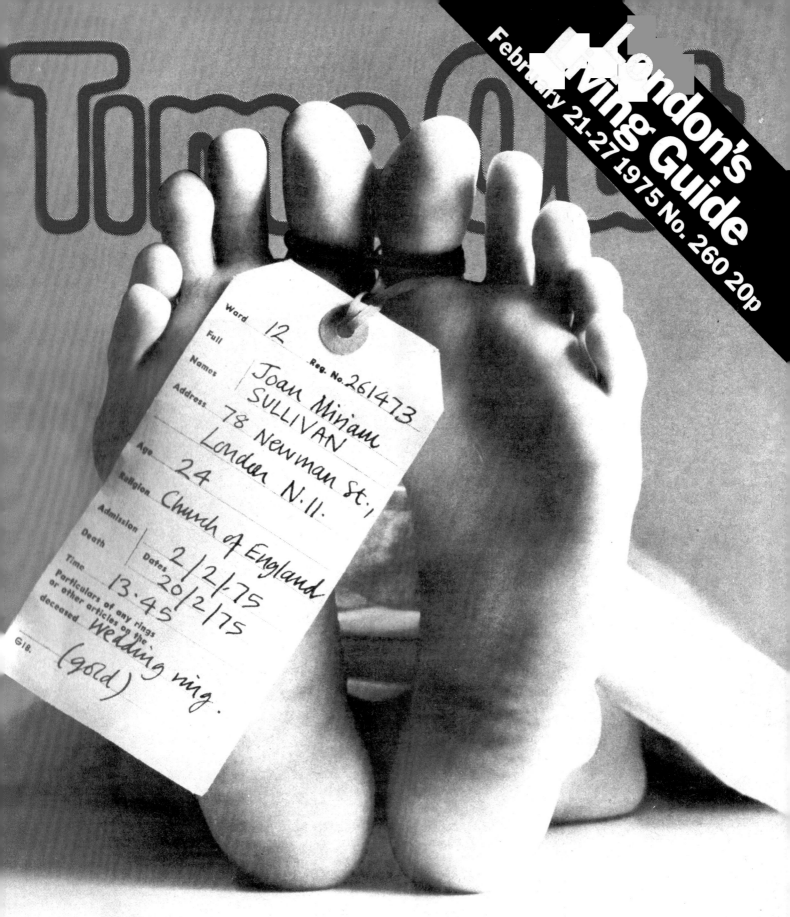

Ward 12 Reg. No. 261473
Full Names Joan Miriam SULLIVAN
Address 78 Newman St. 1
London N. 11.
Age 24
Religion Church of England
Admission
Death Dates 2/2/.75
20/2/75
Time 13.45
Particulars of any rings or other articles on the deceased Wedding ring.
G18. (gold)

86,500 Dead

**Every year this many people die in London.
What happens to them? Inside, we draw back the
coy veil that shrouds London's mortuaries.**

01

02

03

04

→

March 1976
Photography
David James, Roger Perry
Design
Carol Jackson

London boy David Bowie rightfully holds the record for appearing on the most Time Out covers: ten in all, from a 1972 review of his live show in character as Ziggy Stardust to a posthumous tribute issue in 2016. This 1976 cover features a preview of Nic Roeg's Bowie-starring sci-fi vision of America, 'The Man Who Fell to Earth', alongside an interview with the legendary British director.

01 **February 1972**
Design
Jones, Thompson and Ireland

02 **April 1983**
Photography
Chalkie Davies

03 **August 1995**
Photography
Gavin Evans

04 **January 2016**
Photography
Gavin Evans

Time Out

London's ...ving Guide

March 12-18 1976 No.313 25p

Newton's Law: Bowie falls from innocence to earth in Nicholas Roeg's new film — more about sex than science fiction.

'The treasures of London's burgeoning theatre fringe were only revealed to us in this cultural cornucopia. All I learned about London before I lived here was through the pages of Time Out. And I'm still learning.'

Nick Allott, theatre producer

→
November 1977
Design
Pearce Marchbank

Just three months after The King had gone to that rhinestone-clad throne in the sky, a tribute show was about to take to the stage at the new Astoria Theatre in London. Time Out music editor John Collis sat in on the painful open auditions. For the cover (featuring an Andy Warhol-inspired line by editor Richard Williams) designer Pearce Marchbank thought to himself: 'Would you get the part if you looked just like him?'

Time Out

London's Living Guide

Nov 25-Dec 1 1977 No.399 30p

In the future, everybody will be Elvis for 15 minutes.

Jack Good is making dreams come true for P.J. Proby, Shakin' Stevens, and Timothy Whitnall. Cut-out the mask, turn to page 12 and join the club.

'The briefest glance at Time Out confirms that London provides just about every conceivable form of entertainment. There is no better way to review the vast range of amusements that the city has to offer.'

Sir Terence Conran, designer, retailer and restaurateur

→
May 1978
Design
Pearce Marchbank
Photography
Bertrand Polo

'My perfect cover image is a Japanese flag,' says Pearce Marchbank, 'because you've got a huge red blob in the centre of a white space.' Two big cup finals at Wembley in a week, featuring two football teams with red kits (Arsenal v Ipswich in the FA Cup and Liverpool v Club Brugge in the European Cup), gave him the nearest opportunity he got. For that immaculate crimson shine, he took the leather football to a car sprayers' garage.

Time Out

May 5-11 1978 No.422 30p

Red is the colour.

**Clough's Forest having nicked Div. One and the League Cup, can Arsenal and Liverpool make it a
ed flush in this week's FA and European cup finals? Inside, we talk to the men who make them tick.**

'As a teenage arrival from Australia in 1971, Time Out helped me find my way in this new, big city. The Agitprop pages were essential reading for political activists like me, and the news pages gave the best coverage of the new Gay Liberation Front. The pink triangle cover was the first time a non-gay UK publication had given a front cover to a LGBT+ issue and image.'

Peter Tatchell, LGBT+ and human rights activist

→
June 1979
Design
Pearce Marchbank

Time Out has existed for around the same amount of time as the LGBT+ rights movement – and, according to former Gay & Lesbian editor Paul Burston, has always been a first port of call for young queer Londoners searching for community. In his 20-year tenure, from 1993 to 2013, Burston never shied away from writing what he calls 'spiky, angry pieces about things that were wrong'. He also made Time Out one of the first mainstream magazines to feature a trans woman on the cover: 1998 Eurovision winner Dana International.

The magazine that tells you what's on and where to go in London.
June 22-28 1979 No.479 35p

Time Out

A mark of oppression becomes a badge of pride.

London celebrates a decade of Gay Liberation.

'80s

TimeOut

OCTOBER 10-16   WHAT'S ON AND WHERE TO GO

NO.547   SCORE-40P

DON'T PANIC.   THE NEW VIDEO GAMES INSIDE

Inside Time Out

John Fordham

Editor 1978-79 and 1979-81

'Success brought a wider readership and big-budget advertising. The magazine's roots were in the underground press, but Tony Elliott's vision for Time Out was so right for a time of such creative energy, and the young staff were so full of ideas, that it couldn't help but appeal to the mainstream as well as the alternative scene.

Parity of pay helped people to see each other as equals, and avoid a pecking order of "creatives" and everybody else. There'd been one or two major run-ins between staff and editors in the earlier years, and I could see that negotiations rather than diktats were the only way to work. After the dispute over equal pay ended in an impasse in the autumn of 1981, I quit Time Out to edit the cooperatively-run *City Limits*. There was pretty much zero contact between *City Limits* and Time Out staff for a long while afterwards.'

David May

Co-editor 1973-75

'After the four-month strike and shutdown in 1981, Richard Branson intended to grab the Time Out London listings market. He recruited key members of the editorial staff, including Pearce Marchbank, so his *Event* magazine would look like a new-style Time Out. The former strikers were launching *City Limits*, with Ken Livingstone's Greater London Council putting a lot of public money into it, so suddenly London would have three alternative listings magazines. I took leave of absence from my job at the *Sunday Times*, and we helped Tony Elliott to relaunch first and beat the competition.'

←
October 1980
Design
Pearce Marchbank

When comedy editor Malcom Hay investigated the evolution of video games at the outset of the '80s, the cover reminded everyone how it had all started two years before: classic arcade game 'Space Invaders'. 'We did it on a huge bit of board, sticking lots of little prints on a grid,' remembers Pearce Marchbank. 'It was a hell of a lot of work.'

Simon Garfield

Editor 1988-90

'When I joined in 1983, the magazine still hadn't fully recovered from the upheaval of the recent strike over pay and politics, and it had lost some of its radicalism. But it was still a powerful and influential voice in London. There was a growing realisation that readers wanted a reliable steer not just on the best plays, but also on nightlife and shops and alternative culture. Time Out led the way in entertainment and consumer journalism, and we still broke some good investigative stories. The biggest challenge – still true today – was staying relevant to the lives of Londoners.

Simplicity and originality were key to the covers. It also helped if you had the words "Covent Garden" or "Paris" on the cover: those issues consistently outsold everything else. Anything with sex also sold well, as did – shocking as it must seem now – every issue with Tom Cruise on the cover.

My spell at Time Out began as party time: very long lunches, many trips to the restrooms, cocktails in clubs in Covent Garden. The influence of the magazine meant that you'd get invited to some crazy premieres and launches. London was ever-changing, ever-interesting, less clean and globalised and monied than now. It was a city of tribes and opposites, and the clubbing scene was immense. But the party was breaking up by the time I took over as editor in the late '80s, with an economic downturn, the devastations of Aids and the effects of Thatcherism. I think the atmosphere in the office and the magazine reflected that.'

Spike

never less tha...
engaging eno...
of all ages ha...
(Locals: Selec...
Beckenham, ...
Enfield, Epso...
Golders Gree...
Purely. Sutton...
Tottenham, V...
Welling, Woo...
Popeye C...
Porridge ...
1979, Br) Ron...
Beckinsale, F...
Wilde. 95 min...
Better than th...
spin-off' wou...
(WE: Biograp...
The Posse...
**Delaney' (X)...
Pressure' (...
1975, Br) Hert...
James, Frank...
(Locals: Totte...

'One Flew Over the Cuckoo's...

r Live In Concert' at the ... Crazy' currently playing all

Sat 9am-6pm. David Maxwell's specialist French fashion shop is an inspiration for fashion students and designers. Attractions include good woollens, crêpe de Chine, silk chiffons from £20 a yard and some stunning embroidered silk trimmings.

Hair

Coronet Wig 34-36 Wardour St, W1 (437 4836). Open Mon-Sat 10.30am-5.30pm. Coronet Wig is a bizarre Soho institution, dealing in French perfumes and ...

Reggae and more reggae at Daddy Kool.

Daddy Kool 93A Dean St, W1 (... Open Mon-Sat 10am-6pm. ... reggae record ship, with a pa... strong secondhand collection (... well as albums). They have ... board which records reque... collectors.

58 Dean Street Records 58 Dea... (437 4500). Open Mon-Sat 10 ... A marvellous record shop, sp... can buy Japanese imports of ... Wilson records, Morricone...

'The Con Survive'

Five years of gradually increasing police heat on the streets of Brixton inevitably led to the explosion of anger last weekend, argue members of the local community.

Community relations in Lambeth warned:—'The ideas underlying Brixton police methods are more akin to those an army against the community than anything else.'

These methods were masterminded local police commander, Len Adams,

---

Beyond The Law

Almost 200 people were seriously enough injured in the Brixton riot to require hospital treatment. 143 of them were police officers. The most seriously injured was PC Dennis Ozols, still unconscious as we go to press and suffering from a fractured skull.

Some 199 people were arrested, 101 of whom were charged. By Tuesday, 78 of them had appeared in court, nearly all of them remanded on bail on charges ranging from assault, possession of offensive weapons to threatening behaviour and obstruction. Almost all of those charged came from Brixton or its immediate vicinity.

Police vehicles attacked totalled 61, up to Tuesday night with 19 private vehicles damaged or written-off.

Some 26 premises were damaged by fire including three pubs, five houses and two boutiques. In total, 76 shops and homes were seriously damaged (including by fire) during the weekend, and a further 31 shops and houses were slightly damaged.

A police 'thrash' squad: unmarked vans full of plainclothes officers—in truncheons (above). Saturday night in Acre Lane (right).

Flying The Co-op Flag

BRIXTON RIO...

library of '50...
volumes of th...
tures there. I...
bore any rese...
with somethin...
drop for Soho...
fast'.

As Kieron a...
we encounter...
haps more st...
of colour and...
with ease. . .

We found th...
mopolitan en...
stalls, coffee ...
them out.

◁ The bold look i...
Street. Sharp – dig...
most to say the lea...
turned in from Leice...
Square and saw him...
ing by a fruit stall w...
mond's Revue Bar in...
background. There i...

'We have to drag them out now and then. They lose control and start screaming and panicking. It's not a job you write home about, but it has to be done,' he said with mild

---

Never mess with a superhero! 'Superman II' swamps London this week. (Index for venues.)

...ny gave an Oscar for ...ins Taken to Achieve ...rely Visible of Effects, ...n hands down. In it, ...an serves up a faithful ...rsion of the comic strip, ... care taken by his actors ...r as more than cartoon ...matched by his own ... community values and ...occupations of ... the frontier outpost ...tion takes place. If the ...g-up of numerous sight...

Dane, Mic...
To be revi...
(WE: Rialt...
**The Se...
Rio)
**The Se...
(AA) (...
Pullman)...
Holmes)...
**Semio...
**Supressio...
**Serail'...
**The Se...
**Seven...
(Locals: ...
**Sex Er...
(X) (Local...
**Sex Lit...
(X) (Local...
**Sex Ma...
**Shivers...
1974, Can...
Silver, Ly...
87 mins. ...
(Locals...
●'Sid...
**Sex...
Jagle...
Powells...

---

community needs.

The pamphlet proposes a combining of tactics (running a...

---

ill health, and ... subsistence ...tage from the ..., 36 Craven St,...

---

at Beckton on the north and Crossness on the south. This achievement was ahead of its time, but no further interception sewers have been built since 1913.

Evres's dedication to individual choice extend? I asked him whether he supported the legalisation of marijuana. He said: 'We are defending freedom of choice over a legal product, the production of tobacco'.

Like many another rightwing 'freedom fighter', Eyres uses *reductio ad absurdum*: 'Pressure from the State again... smoking is another step along the road to totalitarian dictatorship.' Taking his argument to the other extreme, shouldn't heroin be freely bought and sold? Eyres disagreed.

When I first spoke to Eyres, he claimed that his organisation had no interest in attacking medical evidence of the harmful effects of smoking.

Yet last week he had a letter published in the *Times Health*...

Brixton Suicide

The death of Paul Worrell, an England bantamweight boxer, found hanged in his cell in Brixton prison three days before he was due to be transferred to a hospital ward, was provoked accusations of negligence by the authorities from his relatives and friends.

Worrell was arrested in September after an incident in a Plumstead pub. He was charged with GBH and malicious wounding and placed on remand at Brixton.

Though he had some history of psychiatric illness, found to act, particularly as the stench desperately for the river had become so acute that sheets drenched in disinfectant had to be hung in the House of Commons.

mediate in-patient treatment at Guy's Hospital. But though a bail application was prepared Brixton prison then revised its opinion, saying he was too dangerous to go to a bed that was not a secure bed.

After lengthy delays he was offered a bed at Bethlem hospital from Jan 15. But on January 12 Worrell committed suicide. He hanged himself, his parents were told, between 15-minute checks upon suspected suicide risks.

Worrell had been out of work for some time and in August he had attempted suicide by jumping out of his bedroom window. In Brixton

---

Nightlife: Clubs & Discos
Review

, Alan Opie
e principal roles.
di. Deceptively
n by John
, chorus and
d, but the
een singularly
exception of
ng his ENO
monsaro,
ver the role of
p Collins
ackerras

available) at
s 7.30pm
£1.90-£11.90,

★ **Le Beat Route** 17 Greek St, W1 (734 1470) Piccadilly Circus or Tottenham Court Rd tubes. Admission £3.50m&f. Mon-Sat 9pm-3am.

If the Roxy and the Vortex are names which bring a nostalgic flutter to the hearts of Seditionaries veterans everywhere, then Le Beat Route seems destined for the same legendary status in the annals of the New Romantic movement.

Its Friday night slots are drunken orgies which attract a young and excited crowd, excruciatingly earnest in its slavishness to the weeks trends, and where *NME* hacks can be seen rubbing...

Sister to Peppermint Park, the Grove's pink and brown art deco design and authentic cocktail shakers are pure Hollywood. Food ranges from the sublime to the ridiculous and the music can be annoying if you're out for a tete-a-tete, but the midnight cabaret is usually worth catching.

★ **Dial 9** 32-40 Great Cumberland Place, W1 (723 9284) Marble Arch tube. M/ship £75m, £25f. Admission free for members plus one guest. Other guests £3 Mon-Thur, £4 Fri-Sat. 10pm-3am Mon-Sat. Dress smart.

Strives desperately for the trendy top end of the market but even the fussiness on the door cannot disguise the fact that this is a quiet,...

2812) Har...
m/ship. A...
live rock I...
1am, 2am...
smart.
One of M...
strosities...
are cheap...
there's pk...
hide from...
Boisterou...
I know it'...
decor?? T...
...

---

his clothes. He shopped local.

◁ Eternal Soho — Charcuterie Aubin in Brewer Street. I found its owner ensconsed in her cash room with its giant black telephone next to the bills and receipts held together with a clip like a Red Indian, taking orders for meat and groceries. She's been here, in this beautiful French butchers, for 55 years. Even hep cats have to eat.

△ Sar...
Powells...
where t...
used to r...
shop fror...
of box...
bands, cuff...
sharp suit...
Clothes...
Johnny Danil...
that step w...

Hash House Harriers meet every Fri...
Training Session every Sun...
in Hyde Park. Coached progressive warm-ups. Start ...
ne restaurant. Ask for Tim. All...
Gardens Kruisers meet every Fri...
Kew Gardens Hotel, Sandycombe Rd...
aup 7.30pm; beginners group at...
Further info 940 2220.

'**Time Out has been the heart of London. Before digitisation it was the information for the city, where nothing had existed before.'**

Andrew Logan,
artist and founder of the
Alternative Miss World

→
February 1980
Photography
Red Saunders
Design
Pearce Marchbank

'The culture of people of African descent still wasn't being taken seriously at the time,' says writer and photographer Val Wilmer, whose cover feature explored the political and cultural significance of the reggae movement in the Ladbroke Grove area. 'But Time Out was quite a radical magazine, and very supportive of black culture.' The cover photograph by Red Saunders features prominent London-based reggae artists including Aswad, Brimstone and Sons Of Jah.

The magazine that tells you what's on and where to go in London.
February 29-March 6 1980
No.515 35p

Time Out

Reggae
generation.

Twenty-five years of political music from Ladbroke Grove.

April 1981
Design
Pearce Marchbank
Photography
Brendan Beirne

When Brixton exploded in violence
in 1981, Time Out was caught on
the hop: the planned cover, on
black actors playing Shakespeare,
had to be scrapped. 'We sent an
urgent call out to freelance news
photographers to find a really
punchy riots image,' remembers
picture research assistant Diana
Korchien. The chosen photograph
by Brendan Beirne showed
exhausted policemen in a Brixton
street in the post-riot dawn,
slyly undermining the assertive
quotation by a police spokesman.

The magazine that tells you what's on and where to go in London.
April 17-23 1981 No.574 40p

Time Out

'We control the streets of London and that's all there is to it.'

Metropolitan Police spokesman, April 12 1981.

The weekend that police tactics became London's biggest social problem. Inside. Brixton and beyond...

'If you were a young, middle-class Londoner in the late 1970s and 1980s, Time Out was as vital to your existence as the furniture shop Habitat or the garage where you got parts for your Citroen 2CV.'

Alexei Sayle, comedian and Time Out columnist

→
January 1982
Illustration
Ralph Steadman
Design
Howard Brown

When Lou Stein's stage production of 'Fear and Loathing in Las Vegas' opened in south London, Time Out commissioned Hunter S Thompson himself to write a story. But the writer went on a bender at Time Out's expense and his story (dictated into a cassette recorder) was inaudible. Thompson's old companion, the anarchic artist Ralph Steadman, ended up writing the story as well as creating the cover. 'I decided to do a portrait of Hunter typing, using the word "argh",' the artist remembers. 'He wrote as though he was using the typewriter like a microphone.'

The best selling guide to what's happening in London. January 29-February 4 1982 No. 597 50p

Time Out

Ralph Steadman heads south of the river in search of the real Hunter S. Thompson.

FEAR AND LOATHING IN SW11

→
September 1982
Illustration
Bill Sanderson

Obliterating St Paul's Cathedral
and wiping out the Time Out logo,
Bill Sanderson's terrifying cover
illustration perfectly captures the
nuclear dread that was a constant
background to everyday life in the
early '80s. Inside the issue were
extracts of a new book describing
the catastrophic consequences
of a potential nuclear attack
on London. Like the cover, 'it
manages to make the unthinkable
thinkable,' wrote editor Don Atyeo.

LONDON'S BIGGEST SELLING GUIDE TO FILM · THEATRE · MUSIC · NIGHTLIFE

September 10-16 1982
No. 629 50p

Time Out

London After The Bomb

'WAR WAS DECLARED SEPTEMBER 15.
ON SEPTEMBER 19 THERE WAS AN ATTACK WARNING RED AT 11.55 AM
FOLLOWED BY A FIRST STRIKE BETWEEN NOON AND 12.10...'

'London's communities thread through Time Out's pages: each week a slice of London life is revealed. We used it like a bible for our nightlife activities. One of my greatest thrills was being on the cover in 1984.'

Princess Julia, 'Blitz kid' and London nightlife royalty

→
July 1986
Illustration
David Nelson

In this great period piece from 1986, Time Out went out in the Soho area in search of sleaze, secrets and 'dayowls'. The ever-changing dark heart of the West End still exerted a powerful sense of mystery and intrigue. 'Soho was a perennial favourite with our readers,' remembers editor Don Atyeo. 'The readership was changing to more lifestyle-oriented people, more interested in going out and having a good time than banning the bomb.'

Time Out

LONDON'S WEEKLY GUIDE   JULY 2-8 1986   No.828   80p

VISITORS GUIDE INSIDE

SOHO

The People, Places And Strange Secrets Of London's Black Mile

- Ronnie Scott
- Strippers
- Nightbirds
- Dayowls
- Clubs
- Cafés
- Shops
- Restaurants
- & Much More

Win Queen Tickets For Wembley

TimeOut

London's weekly guide
May 18-25 1994 No.1239 £1.50

SPECIAL ISSUE

THE HIGHS AND LOWS OF DRUGS

Complete
8-day
TV
guide

Inside Time Out

←
May 1994
Design
Jeremy Leslie
Photography
Richard Dean

With a regular focus on sex and rock 'n' roll, it's no surprise that Time Out has also devoted more than a few covers to drugs. This 1994 issue was certainly provocative, but it was a serious in-depth look at the subject, intended to counter Nancy Reagan's 'Just say no' campaign in the US. The cover, according to art director Jeremy Leslie, was 'the only time I've managed to claim drugs on expenses'.

Dominic Wells

London editor 1992-98

'The '90s were a felicitous time for British culture. Britpop, the YBAs, 'Trainspotting': there was an extraordinary flourishing in British creative arts of all kinds. The restaurant scene in the capital was also changing fast. It was one of the best periods for London as a creative city since the 1960s.

The Time Out office was full of fantastically bright, talented, eccentric, driven people, and the atmosphere was one of creative chaos. There were tonnes of smokers, and we'd often get in drinks if people were working late. The pace of creating a weekly magazine that was 220 pages long – basically the same size as a monthly – was relentless. Editing Time Out was the most challenging, aggravating, exhausting thing – but most of all, it was sheer fun.

The staff were super-experts in their fields. The film editor, the theatre editor or the music editor absolutely lived and breathed the subject that they covered. Whatever question you had to ask, they knew the answer. Whatever kind of industry contact that you needed, they would not only know them, they would've been out drinking with them until four o'clock in the morning.

One of the biggest changes in the '90s was introducing full colour throughout the whole magazine. Before that, you had four pages of colour in the features and the listings were just a wash of grey. When we finally worked out the production niggles, it lifted the whole magazine.

Tony Elliott always used to say that the cover is the poster of the magazine. When the marketing department was asking for more money, he'd always say, "We don't need to market Time Out: it's there on the newsstands." So you had to see the cover as a piece of advertising, and not just a piece of content. I would scrutinise the sales figures like a Roman soothsayer scrutinising the entrails of birds. Guides to things like Camden or cheap eats always sold well. Covers with sex on them pretty much always sold out, so much so that I took a risk and did one two weeks before Christmas, when no one was buying magazines, and it still sold out.

People that are famous just for being famous don't necessarily work on the cover of Time Out. Arnold Schwarzenegger would always bomb: even though he was the biggest star in the world, Time Out readers just weren't interested. But if you put Chloë Sevigny on the cover – someone who was cooler and a bit more arty – or one of the new British stars, then that would work.'

Laura Lee Davies

London editor 1998-99 and 1999-2004

'We were doing bigger issues than ever before, and entertainment news was speeding up so competition was tighter. We had 40-plus full-time staff and about 30 more part-timers. The brilliant thing about working with creative people is that they all have strong opinions and ideas. The downside is that every time you want to change anything, you have to have even stronger opinions and even better ideas than every single one of them. It was knackering.

London was the party city at the heart of "Cool Britannia". The office on Tottenham Court Road was just too handy a distance from late-night drinking in Soho, we had 24-hour access to the office and the sofas on the top floor were very big. The morning after one particular awards ceremony, I remember signing out of the office to go and get breakfast as everyone else was arriving for work.

Mobile phones changed things. Once people could change plans with a call, Londoners became more fickle: they didn't need to think ahead. The magazine was getting bigger but people were too busy to read something that cost more than £3 every week, let alone do half the things it told them about. It was time to evolve.'

rest for the

like fuck?' enquires an ard... Meanwhile, an Irish guy tries recruit Lisa's significant other band, he tells her for a porn

..., Stephan Talty.

...& Opera Tom Samijan
etc. Gail O'Hara (Editor)
...Leander Williams, Robin Eisgrau

...nberg (Editor), Sam Whitehead

...rs Cathay Che, Stephin Merritt,
...r Peter Wells

...n de la Peña
...r Rommel Aloma

...r Kelli Thompson
...nda Laing

...Director Ayad Sinawi
...ner Bonnie Snellen
...ms Coordinator Pete Curtner

...Director Alison Tocci
... Representatives
...nn, Christian Gregory, Dan
...a, Anne Perton, Siobhan Shea
...ction Coordinator

Page 23 Sighs and Vespas: Here's how and where to join the latter-day mod squad.

takeout

2 Film I want my pre-MTV! 1,000 ultra-cheesy '60s videos.
Theater All possible worlds collide in the new *Candide*.
Art She's young, she's sexy—she's eight years old?
Music Altered in the States: *I Could Be Happy* arrives.

features

6 Mary, quite contrary
Hip-hop diva Mary J. Blige bares her soul (kind of).

12 Twilight zone

114 **Music:** Classical & Opera
118 **Sports**
120 **Theater:** Reviews
With discount ticket information.
123 **Theater:** Broadway
125 **Theater:** Off Broadway
129 **Theater:** Off-Off
Broadway
133 **Travel**
Time In
134 **Television**
136 **Radio**
137 **Video**
138 **Byte Me**
140 **Classified &**
Personals
143 **Ask Isadora**
144 **Free Stuff**
Go see
Whoopi,
hear the
new *Lolita*
or win a
Yak*Pak.

write in

irrevocably wounded, for we could have been friends. No love and no sincerity and no more *Time Out* for you.
—Blossom Dearie, Manhattan

B one up on the it has to be co **bone marrow** is th one of the archite tribute with StJoh and soft inside an sandwiched betw

Liverpool boss's quote: 'The socialis believe in is everyo working for each oth Everyone having a share of the reward. It's the way I see life.' Let's hope sal don't bomb, as with the Klinsmann shirt

BAR WARS
After the Boo Radle gig at the Astoria, t Burgess? Our Tim popsters retreated an after-gig thrash nearby nightspot. O who invited Tim Charlatans? Our Tim Perryman a less risky y shirt on 16.25, he ex-

EAT OUT

Critics' picks
Eat outings See
Just opened Vo

But what, "Gefilte" liter in Yiddish an tional of prep water fish tha carp skin. Now ply molded in using matzo, poached in f commonly us pike. The dish

In every re was essentially soning. Jews (Litvaks) pref ened; Jews of ferred it swee

Few people days—the fir is very expe messy and in jars, made from Mother many a gefilt ders on sacrifi

Londonbeat News

The week in brief
Last week's news in review

A LONDON MAN was so upset that a Cornish pasty he bought failed to live up to expectations, he complained to the Advertising Standards Authority. He claimed the pasty he had seen on a poster ad was deeper and more densely filled than the one he had eaten. But the advertising firm concerned, BBH Unlimited, sent a till receipt to prove the pasty they had used

A self-confessed gang murderer-turned-auth... announced plans to stan London Mayor. Dave Cou inspiration for Vinnie Jon character in 'Lock, Stock... Smoking Barrels' and an friend of the Krays, has s that if he is elected he wo like Jeffrey Archer as his ro 'Anyone who can come up alibis as good as Archer's

Gay
Preview

Hero to heroin

Paul Burston on Boy George

Fame, as David Bowie once warned, 'puts you there where things are hollow'. Boy George ought to know. Back in the days when he ranked as the greatest living tabloid sensation, George was famous for three things: looking like a big girl's blouse, saying he'd sooner have a nice cup of tea than a good shag, and providing fat girls from the suburbs with a role model.

Of course this was all before he got smacked out of his head on heroin. By the time the fat fell off, and Georgie Porgie was revealed as Junkie George, the girls didn't want to be like him anymore. They wanted to be like Madonna. Like the song says, 'is it any wonder?'

Nowadays, George is fond of reminding us that 'style and content are inseparable', that just as 'Ziggy was more than his stardust', he was always more than the sum of his eyebrows, buttons and bows.

In a sense, he is right. Of all the club queens who slipped into the pop mainstream shortly before the mid '80s AIDS panic, George was the one who came closest to true superstardom. His is the face that launched a dozen hits, give or take the odd underground club anthem. Some, like 'Time', 'Church of the Poison Mind' and 'Generations of Love', are the sorts of songs people of a certain generation will probably take to the grave. Others, like 'Karma Chameleon', 'The War Song' and 'Bow Down Mister' are more likely to have been given away to the local charity shop.

But it is for the nature of his celebrity, rather than the qualities of his music, that the Boy Wonder is destined to be remembered. It seems entirely fitting, then, that his long-awaited autobiography should

Ooh, saucy! Submission start off the Easter weekend with a decadent bang at their Hot Cross Fun do on Thursday, when Paul Oakenfold joins the party.

...leaders

...ted alphabetically. On the ...he week - Wed to Sat - ...d by types of music and ...tically. Venue addresses ...uded with the listing in *Nightlife* ...l order in the listings. ...we recommend. ...ver – admission is free! ...mission is available on ...issue of *Time Out*. ...This club is open after

...d is available. ...e range is mentioned, this ...**rage age** of clubbers at an ...age limit. ...Unless otherwise stated. ...ode.

...contributors

...ve in writing by 5pm on ...ys before publication (NB: ...ore the date of the event). ...mission prices, times. ...d a contact phone number. ...nt by post or by fax (0171 ...ngs are free, but inclusion ...due to limited space. ...erning regular clubs will be ...ues and then dropped

Always attracts long queues of phunky-phabulous clubbers, so dress up and get down *early* if you wanna rumble to Brian Norman and Misbehaviour's mix of G-funk, Hip Hop and underground Garage on the balconied main floor or groove in the Funky Room below where Lloydy, Maura Miller and Ben & Pete get

David & Russ spin Duranies & Blondie to Madonna on the main floor at this packed '80 night while John plays poptastic & indie clas sics down in the crypt. Arrive before 11.30pm o it'll be ram-jammed. Age: 18-40-something.
Sol Y Sombra Cuba, W8. 9pm-2am; £3.
DJs Dave Hucker & Martin Morales mix go

of the foot which is really sexy, and the matt red colour is perfect.
Vivienne Westwood, 43 Conduit St, W1 (0171 439 1109) Oxford Circus tube. Open Mon-Sat 10am-6pm, Thur 10am-7pm.

strapping on this sandal is clever and intricate. It gives the impression that the shoe has been tied to the foot – a bit like Roman sandals, but fine, delicate and sophisticated. Very ingenious!'.
Gina, 189 Sloane Street, SW1 (0171 235 2932) Knightsbridge tube. Open Mon-Sat 10am-6pm, Wed 10am-7pm.

courts (Fetish Range) £29.99
'A lot of people d this basic shoe shape but very few do it any better than this and for £29.99 you can't beat them. I really like the pointed toe o this shoe, which is very difficult to get right. They are well finished, the leather is nice, and the heel is properly strengthened. It' a great basic, sexy shoe.'
Shellys, 266-270 Oxford St, W1 (0171 287 0939 Oxford Circus tube. Open Mon-Sat 10am-7pm, Thurs 10am-8pm Sun 10am-6pm. See phone book for branches.

...orenzo, black suede ...ce trim stiletto with ...orset fastening ...mechanism £25
...Whoever created this ...hoe must have been ...ompletely mad. The ...idea of incorporating ...is complicated, lacy ...suspender-belt into a ...shoe and for it to ...actually work is ...amazing.'
...Julia Chettati, ...Portobello Road ...Market, Portobello ...Green, W11 (0956 ...243634) Ladbroke ...Grove tube. Open Fri, ...Sat 8.30am-6pm.

JAD Paris, blue metallic strappy stiletto sandal with coiled-wire heel detail £55
'These are real dress-up, good-time shoes – perfect for a disco They still have a certain cheap-hooker quality, but they're still really nice. The wired leg coil is really clever and cool, and again the exposed flesh is really sexy.'
Julia Chettati, as before.

Sell out

Where they eat
Geeta Patel designer

A year out of Central St Martins, Geeta Patel was designing a collection for Whistles and Pellicano which walked out of the shops in a few weeks. It hasn't gone to her head or her stomach, and she eschews the fashionable feeding spots of the West End. 'I've heard of Quaglino's, but why would I want to go there?' she asks. 'Maybe if someone else was paying... Though she lives and works

Le Creole Cajun

Being bang opposite Brixton tube up an alley doesn't seem to be as advantageous for this restaurant as it is for the buzzing Brixtonian one street up. So the aim at Le Creole is clearly to attract the punters by whatever means necessary: live acoustic guitar music, a long list of cocktails; a couple of pasta dishes and sandwiches; make it up for the Fridays, a sign-postured by a card by the Fridays, they're still nice supposed inducements only detract from the thing the place does really well and should concentrate on: Cajun food.

Our evening begins unpromisingly with cocktails, steep, at £4.95. A 'margarita' is made with Pernod. On sending it back we're told, apologetically, 'We're out of tequila' and asked whether we'd mind vodka instead. We decide fancy drinks are not their forte, and order wine. Our choice is unavailable. The same goes for some items on their highly imaginative menu. For this, and their horrible plastic tablecloths, they are forgiven—especially when the food arrives.

'Shallow Grave'
Kerry Fox, Christo-
gor. Ken Stott. 92

flatmate suffers a
d Juliet find a for-
p his room. They
honey, but nothing
re involves not only
out the trio's trust,
impressively as-
ritish feature does-
play has the kind of
m and close-to-the-
h sees you safely
minefields, even if
ir in retrospect. A
only more British

REENINGS
(071 608 0125) M'-
50. Annual m'ship

(Terror at the
to Christina
ano Barberini,
...ian.

of Subversive
'Great', etc. For
n 0181 830 3145.
sion £3, members

ichmond (081 892
ear £15.
dding Banquet'
5) Winston Chao,
Subtitled. 107

ect: a Taiwanese in
estate, and shares
-term white lover
he hasn't come
om Taiwan of their
nstall an arranged
enant Wei-Wei, a
een Card, to join in
ce. Then his par-
g for the wedding.
ronising his char-
omedy both subtle
otive social asides:
ion amid the jokes,
ks a real emotion

OURSES

3) Bethnal Green.
ear £15.
) Films
y; £280, concs

anodyne romantic at least it's a good slackly at first, but and DeVito is orator Dr Arbo-

Neeson, Ben Goodall. 195

neally's novel is his editing and grainy As surprising as piction of brutal andle actors – Nee- profiteer whose use Jews from death; canny Jewish ac- urderous comman- eeks to simplify the ndler. As in his ear- der at the inexplic- a scream of horror

wilightzone

...ctor Christopher Reeve raves about the actor's performanc... HBO film, but Robert Sean Leonard may be happiest onsta...

...o Motoyama Photographed by **François Dischinger**

...fter his career-making turn as the ...doomed young thespian in 1989's *Dead*

busy man. Let me break this down for you: Are you a model?" Leonard said he was not. "Do you

The actor, who live... proven himself rath...

food & drink

9 PERSON TASTE TEST · KOSHER WEEKLY · SINCE 1995 · MAY BE USED FOR PASSOVER · Time Out New York

'Time Out's covers made it as important as *Rolling Stone* if you lived in the city, and film and cultural icons were a big part of its impact. Countless Londoners have been stimulated by its influential recommendations, me included.'

Jeremy Thomas,
film producer

→
April 1994
Design
Jeremy Leslie and Kirk Teasdale
Photography
Terry O'Neill

Two years after 'Absolutely Fabulous' launched, the actress Joanna Lumley's popularity was as high as her hairdos. When approaching the cover design, art director Jeremy Leslie recalls, 'The editor and I would chat over a few pints in the pub. After mostly talking a load of rubbish, we'd come up with a clever idea. The Warhol design isn't original, but we wanted to play with the idea of Joanna being an icon and having her 15 minutes of fame.'

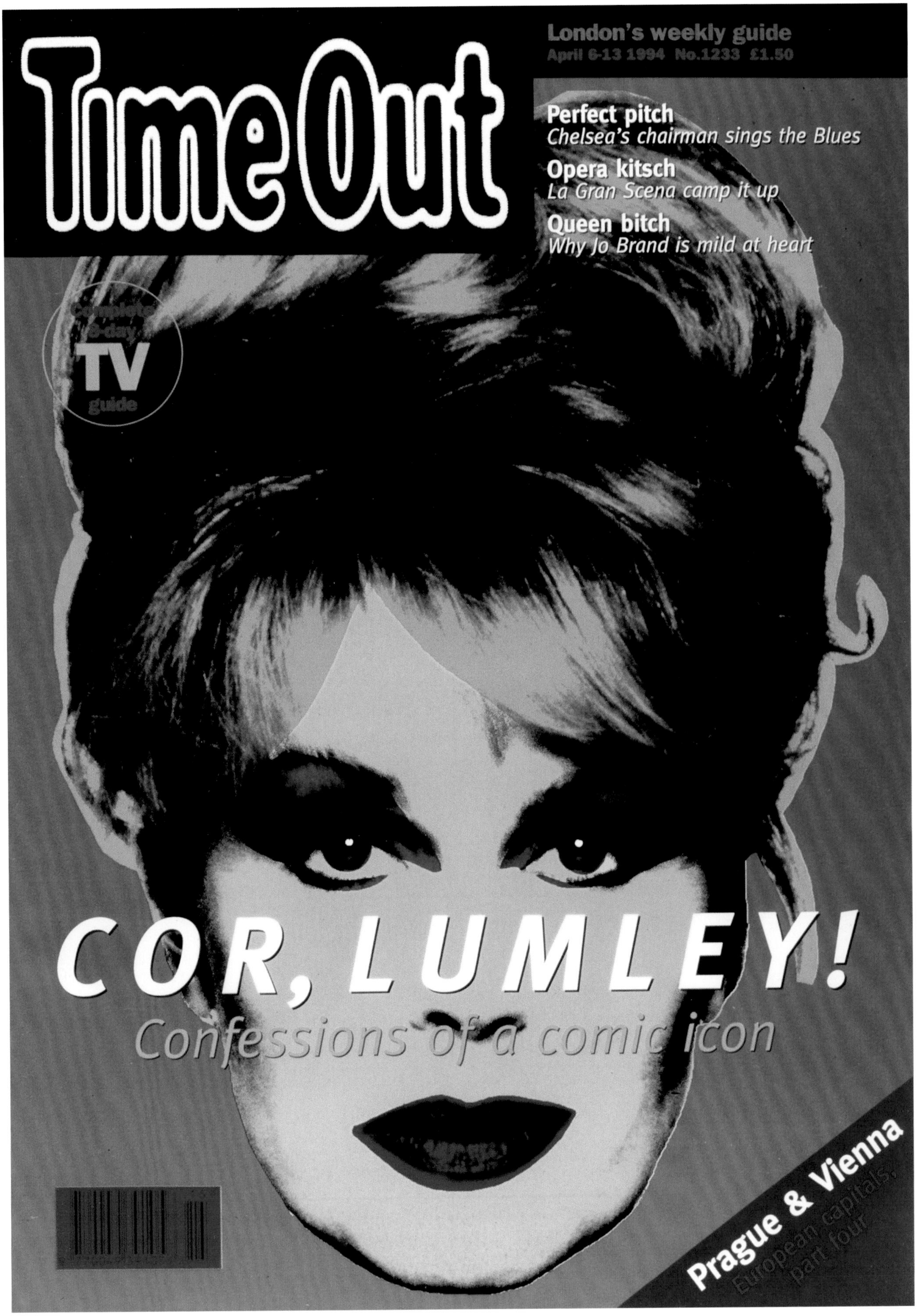

Time Out

London's weekly guide
April 6-13 1994   No.1233   £1.50

Perfect pitch
Chelsea's chairman sings the Blues

Opera kitsch
La Gran Scena camp it up

Queen bitch
Why Jo Brand is mild at heart

Complete
8-day
TV
guide

COR, LUMLEY!

Confessions of a comic icon

Prague & Vienna
European capitals,
part four

'I shot quite
a lot of covers
for Time Out and
met lots of great
people in wonderful
places. I wouldn't
have made it half
this far without the
faith placed in me.'

Perou, music and fashion
photographer

→
April 1998
Photography
Perou

Time Out has helped launch
many photographers' careers,
including that of Perou – who
remembers this cover as the
start of his 20-year collaborative
friendship with the rock star
Marilyn Manson. 'It amused
me that this Easter cover with
the line "Jesus Christ!" didn't
get letters, but another Easter
cover I did for Time Out, with
David Beckham wearing rosary
beads, had a bishop writing in
to complain.'

Time Out

London's living guide
April 8-15 1998 No.1442 £1.80

Neil Tennant
On Noel Coward's London
Clubbed to death!
Our 24-hour Sunday marathon

Plus
30-page
TV
guide

Easter exclusive

Jesus Christ!

Who the hell does Marilyn Manson think he is?
Enter the weird world of music's mad messiah

PLUS Our divine guide to London's churches

→
April 1995
Illustration
Jamie Hewlett

The screen adaptation of
'Tank Girl' was nothing like the
subversive original comic: it
was so crap that Time Out's film
editors refused to cover it. But
editor Dominic Wells, who began
his career in comics journalism,
saw a cover story: Jamie Hewlett,
the strip's creator, was unusually
vocal about his hatred for it. 'We
allowed him to do what he wanted
with his cover illustration,' says
Wells. 'Once we had that striking
image, the cover lines wrote
themselves.'

'Good old Time Out – the internet pre-internet. All that information, all those brilliant events I went to because of it. Thanks for all the fun times.'

Rankin, music and fashion photographer

'When I first arrived in London, Time Out was my indispensable guide to London's galleries, bookshops, markets, cafés and theatres. I am pretty certain that is how I first discovered The Photographers' Gallery. Time Out has always supported independent and emerging venues, and London life is richer because of it.'

Brett Rogers, director of The Photographers' Gallery

→
December 1996
Photography
Lillie Curry

Amid a mid-'90s landscape of smutty lads' mags, editor Dominic Wells wanted to show that sexuality was all shades of 'weird' – and imported the US idea of the split cover to do just that. Four different covers were picked by art director Kirk Teasdale from more than 100 images contributed for free by artists and photographers, including art photographer David LaChapelle. This one was credited to Lillie Curry – Teasdale's granny.

Time Out

London's weekly guide
December 4-11 1996 No.1372 £1.70

WARNING!
The explicit nature of some material may cause offence

Complete
8-day
TV
guide

Weird Sex

Are you missing out? Our sensational survey and photo gallery reveal all

SPECIAL ISSUE
.2 in a series of 4 covers

Xmas Xxxtra
Sexy lingerie to
wear if you dare

→
Time Out New York, September 1995
Photography
Troy Ward

'Welcome to New York. Now get out' was one of the cheeky phrases that covered NYC to announce the arrival of Time Out's first magazine outside of London. 'We wanted to convey our youthful enthusiasm but also our New York attitude,' remembers founding editor Cyndi Stivers. 'Most people thought we were crazy and gave us no chance, but I knew we could make each issue a party, and our readers agreed.' The new magazine's circulation would eventually outstrip that of Time Out London.

The complete weekly guide
September 27–October 4, 1995 Issue No. 1 $1.95

Time Out

New York

ALL-NIGHT NEW YORK

les from the dark side
us a full roundup
24-hour services
d entertainment

Mira Sorvino,
star of Woody Allen's
Mighty Aphrodite

'00s

Time Out

London's living guide
March 14-21 2001 No.1595 £2.20

TIM BUCKLEY
FUN LOVIN' CRIMINALS
LAURA LINNEY
THE PRISONER
CITIBANK PHOTO PRIZE

36-PAGE TV SECTION

DON'T HAVE A COW, MAN'
VEGETARIAN SPECIAL FOR LONDON'S CONFIRMED CARNIVORES

COVER: ALAN MAHON

9 770049 391100

Inside Time Out

If this gore-splattered vegetarian special makes you recoil, then you've reacted exactly as art director Balwant Ahira intended. 'There was a big movement towards vegetarianism at the time, as a result of the spread of foot-and-mouth disease in the UK,' he says. 'Being a vegetarian myself, I felt that this was the time for me to really make a point and shock people.' The result: a cover that is as stylish as it is subversive, achieved using nothing but a meat cleaver and a tomato.

Laura Lee Davies

London editor 1998-99 and 1999-2004

'Time Out is London, for better or worse – whether fighting off the bulldozers at a new development or getting way too excited about a new food trend. Pick up any issue over the last 50 years and you don't just get a snapshot of London history at that time, the passion, obsessions and humour of Londoners at that moment leap out at you too. In the days before mobile phones could do much more than look like bricks and make crackly calls, we were social media.

I knew from my time as music editor that each section was like an entire magazine in itself. You were never just chipping in to something bigger: every section was able to stand alone as a great read. We had to have great film covers and music covers, because we were a great film magazine and a great music magazine. Every Time Out cover should define something about what Time Out is.

Weirdly, online hasn't been the death of live entertainment. The "be here now", "taste this now", "do this now" moment has made more people want to get out and enjoy London. That filters into the buzz of what the magazine is today.'

Gordon Thomson

London editor 2004-09

'The Time Out office was a vibrant, fun, extraordinarily febrile and occasionally quite drunken place: a world where anything was possible. Print sales were declining in the wake of newspapers starting to publish free "going out" listings, but the magazine remained fiercely independent and the editor still had a huge amount of power: it was a time when you could pretty much do what you wanted to without interference. That was entirely down to Tony Elliott.

I was very young and basically winging it – I'm amazed I got away with it for so long. (I still can't believe I didn't get turfed out for printing a cover entirely in Arabic.) We felt that Time Out was a political animal as well as a conduit for bringing great entertainment to Londoners, and that it should have a strong political voice. Londoners expected Time Out not just to be a meek guide to entertainment but to have a view on issues. My Time Out had no truck with pointless celebrity and an unashamed south London bias. I did enjoy making north London sweat for every column inch.'

...get cancer,' wrote ...e *Time Out* web-...

Photograph: Tom Howard

PLUGGED IN

Art

Stuck in the middle

Now Display of ...s by 20 designers ...ndent labels between ...g Duckie Brown, ...Sep 2.
...seniors £7, ...ibition focusing on ...alism through ...bits are Elsa ...d Dali's Lobster ...im's Table With ... Art
...ths Exploring the ...n on art and design, ...ary artists including ...ichael Paul Britto are ...he museum alongside ...► Jun 17.
...rivate Buildings, ...ties *June 11 8pm; ...* Talk by the ...e Pompidou, New ...w World Trade ...yd's Building and ...ers will explore the ...of balancing the ...the institution, the

Ossian Ward talks to Tracey Emin about why she's proud to represent Britain at the Venice Biennale but is equally at home on 'Wogan'

'My ego is insane.' The first words to come out of Tracey Emin's mouth should come as no surprise to those familiar with the artist's self-loathing and self-centred practice. Since bursting onto the YBA art scene in the 1990s with her autobiographical embroidered quilts, neon scribbles and live nude painting performances, she has quite literally traded on her own identity and, more recently, on her new-found celebrity. Twenty years after her short-lived personal pantheon the Tracey Emin Museum opened on Waterloo Road (funded through a system of bonds redeemable against works of art), her handwriting has almost become a currency in its own right and her distinct flourishing signature, some would say, is a license to print money.

Her name, now a commodity too, is more often associated with the pages of glossy magazines than with serious art journals and her sponsors are not just galleries like White Cube and collectors like Charles Saatchi but fashion houses such as Longchamp, for whom she designed a limited-edition 'International Woman' suitcase in 2004. She has her own newspaper column and recently published her memoirs to date, the disturbing but pleasurable book 'Strangeland'. Yet her iconic status is...

Out There

Unorthodox approach

Hadassah Gross has the chutzpah to bring...

...o animal rights activism than chasing fox-hunters across ...elling at livestock trucks. And now would-be protesters ...ses to equip themselves with all the skills necessary for...

...st and survive

Another must-have for the serious sabber is a gizmo. First used in the 1960s, when organised sabbing started in earnest, it is a Walkman-based sound system through which the noises of hounds on the scent of their quarry are amplified. 'If the dogs hear this, they'll think another pack of hounds has found something. They'll come haring to where you're replaying...

Talkin...

The illustrated g...
By **Bob Eckstein**

...t's that time of ...song you hear s ...a new record o... Elton John, Brian ...

Venues

Nightlife

...s not nu-rave, it's a new wave!

...trends move so ...ey're often a blur, ...re's a new league of ...c mash-up DJ royalty ...ng from the East End ...that are here to stamp ...evil-may-care 'tude ...bbers in the capital. ...e Hutchinson. ...graphy **Rob Greig**.

...Disco Squad *The elite ravers ...y nine members strong, ZDS ...as and Nat scaled down to a ...in 2005 and now slay the floor ...nthly East End night Get ...e've turned down gigs because ...want to be associated with hype; ...ve're more substance over style. ...house-tempo music but mix in ...k and Baltimore club music, ...ing heavy basslines and ...with a lot of bounce.' ...em* at Get Rude at Catch on ...9 and Bastard Soundsystem at ...nic on June 10.

...ice *The Erol protegées ...mention fresh talent without ...Ben. They've been working ...h into a frenzy for years with ...-heavy mixes, drawing praise ...Alkan and MSTRKRFT. 'We ...f listening to Erol, 2ManyDJs ...no, and playing house parties. It ...f from there. Fave tracks at the ...The new Hot Chip single and ...Dat" by Mark Aaran.' ...em* at Walk The Night at ...June 14 and Adventures in the ...Field at Fabric on June 15.

...ell Out *The new superstar DJ ...ung-gun Tommy Bisdee has ...raced the cover of *DJ* and will ...masses with his Mark Ronson ...ove rerubs this summer. 'I'm ...ing the new British dance ...ull Juice, Sinden, Herve, Switch ...going to completely take over. ...y ammunition? I've got party ...an air horn, a big nose and a ...glossy, nostalgic electro.' ...m* at Herbal on July 14 and at ...Lovebox Weekender on July 22.

...onix *The girl/boy duo ...and Manara have only been ...together for three months but ...ady notched spots at Modular

Zombie Disco Squad

Skull Juice

Kissy Sell Out

Coconut Twins

tapedeck

eLPL...

My Favourite Londoner

...n Letts on ...e Moss

...choice might seem a bit weird ...ople who know me – or think ...ow me – but contrary to popular ...x, being earnest and worthwhile. ...softer side, and occasionally I'm

...we have a lot of mutual friends – and what you see is pretty much what you get. She's amazingly frank and she's got a level head. She's a south London girl, and I'm a south London guy myself, so I know her kind of mentality.

Kate's proved to be a muse to designers, musicians, photographers... And Lucian Freud – here's a woman who's been...

→
January 2000
Art director
Kirk Teasdale

How to make the most of your money in a pricey city is a recurring Time Out theme. This particular take pastiched the cheap-and-cheerful classified adverts found in most publications at the time. 'Many people might not remember classifieds, but they were essential for Londoners to find anything from new restaurants to the love of your life,' says editor Laura Lee Davies. 'I also like the way the art director sneaked in our other features around the sides.'

'I can't imagine London without Time Out. It's a must for anyone who's interested in the arts, culture and everything going on in London. Long may it continue.'

Twiggy, fashion icon

Time Out

London's living guide
January 19-26 2000 No.1535 £1.95

HOT SOFA ACTION!
TV and listings for the next 8 days

DRAMA KING
Why Paul Abbott is the new Jimmy McGovern

JOHN HURT
on the light side of Beckett's darkness

Richard Fea...
from Death in Vega...

'LON...
LI...

Painti...
Decora...
No Jo...
Sm...

SAVE! SAVE! SAVE!

£ CHEAP £ LONDON

- ★ **FOOD!**
- ★ **ELECTRONICS!**
- ★ **BOOKS!**
- ★ **HOUSEHOLD!**
- ★ **ENTERTAINMENT!**
- ★ **EATING OUT!**

How to have a night on the town for free!

WIN! GET YOUR HANDS ON SOME FUNKY MP3 GEAR!

'Time Out was my bible. It used to be the only way to navigate cultural experiences in London, and the exhibition and film reviews were always spot on.'

Amanda Levete, Stirling Prize-winning architect

→
January 2002
Photography
Tony Gibson

Any Londoner will be familiar with the sight of grubby white transit vans like this one, gracing a cover that was partly inspired by Pet Shop Boys' grimy London-set music video for 'Home and Dry'. 'We decided to give the city a health check,' says editor Laura Lee Davis, 'covering everything from air pollution to rat-infested pubs to poo in swimming pools.' The dirty white van was the perfect

Time Out

London's living guide
January 23-30 2002 No.1640 £2.20

DIRTY LONDON

**Recycle!
Give up smoking!
Discover the truth about London's grimy greatness!**

Transit

P237 MVX

Brian Wilson
Surf's up at the South Bank

Marti Pellow
'I'd much rather sing to ladies
than a bunch of hairy-arsed guys'

Martin Parr
Voyeur or visionary?

WIN
A QUAGLINO'S CHEF FOR VALENTINE'S DAY
**A WIDESCREEN TV,
DVD PLAYER AND HI-FI**

LONDON'S WEEKLY LISTINGS BIB
NOVEMBER 17-24 2
No.1787 £2

Time Out

London

SUPERSTAR GUEST EDITOR

ELTON'S THE BOSS

And I demand…

Tom Wolfe
U2
Tom Waits
Naomi Klein
The 20 best
albums of the year
The poshest Hamlet
Watford
**A sackful of singles
to review!**

+

**My Christmas
shopping
secrets
revealed**

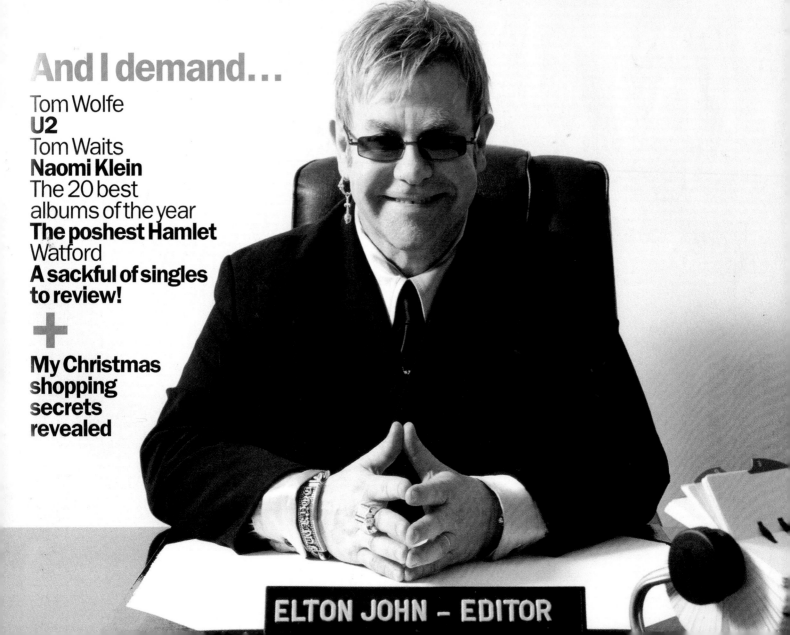

ELTON JOHN – EDITOR

AND YOU KNOW WHAT ELTON'S LIKE WHEN HE DOESN'T GET HIS WAY

←
November 2004
*Photography
Rob Greig*

Time Out has had many guest editors, but none more famous than Sir Elton John, who appeared on both sides of a gatefold cover. 'We wanted a big name to make a splash,' explains actual editor Gordon Thomson, 'and we liked the idea of him sitting behind an austere desk with his crappy name badge in a crummy Time Out office. The reality was nowhere near that: although Elton did select the stories that went into the magazine, I'm ashamed to say he never set foot in the building.'

ELTON JOHN – EDITOR

'Time Out is to this city what the ravens are to the Tower of London: it's hard to imagine the capital without it. The breadth of content, humour, unforgiving scrutiny of political figures and curiosity about everything cultural makes it a consistently brilliant read. And I've always loved the "Overheard in London" column: you can find true wisdom in there.'

Munira Mirza, former deputy mayor for education and culture

→
July 2005
Art director
Micha Weidmann

On the morning of July 7 2005, four suicide bombers detonated explosions on tube trains and a bus. Fifty-two Londoners were killed. 'We were due to go to press that day with a bubbly summer preview,' remembers editor Gordon Thomson, 'and we had only a few hours to come up with a new cover. We felt very strongly that London wouldn't be cowed by these bombings, so we came up with this simple, unapologetic message. At the vigil in Trafalgar Square that week, it was very moving to see people holding copies of this cover up as a sign of defiance.'

LONDON'S WEEKLY LISTINGS BIBLE
JULY 13-20 2005
No.1821 £2.50

OUR CITY

LONDON CARRIES ON

'Time Out's encouragement and recognition had a huge impact on the creative life of the capital. We take it for granted now – my children find the idea of life before Time Out as weird as life before the mobile phone – but it was a glorious breakthrough.'

Jude Kelly, artistic director of the Southbank Centre

→
June 2007
Art director
Nick Booth

Amid fear and controversy about Islamic extremism, Time Out decided to make a powerful statement about the importance of London's Islamic community. The resulting cover attracted plenty of attention – it was widely praised and condemned both in London and across the world. 'Looking back, I'm not sure we got it right,' says editor Gordon Thomson. 'It was definitely the worst selling issue during my editorship.' But it remains one of the most memorable and controversial Time Out covers since the 1970s.

Time Out London

LONDON'S WEEKLY LISTINGS BIBLE
JUNE 6 – 12 2007
No.1920 £2.50

هل مستقبل لندن إسلامي؟

Is London's future Islamic?

KNOW MORE.
DO MORE.
August 18 – 24 2011
timeout.com/london

£3.25
No.2139

#ilove london

The greatest city in the world bounces back

Inside Time Out

Tim Arthur

London editor 2011-13 and CEO 2013-2015

'I joined Time Out just after they banned drinking and smoking pot at your desk. By the time I became editor, London was in a golden period. The lead-up to the 2012 Olympics kicked off a whole period of London pride. There was an explosion of cultural and gastronomic talent. There were more great restaurants than Paris and more exciting dive bars than New York. I got to travel the world with Time Out to see other great cities, but London genuinely was the most exciting city on the planet at that time.

However, we were under huge strain financially. The new internet monoliths had started to suck in all media advertising spend, changing the whole landscape that we'd operated in for 40-odd years. Fewer and fewer people were prepared to buy magazines, established print brands were closing on a weekly basis and everything was moving online. Within a week of my becoming editor, the CEO sat me down and basically told me we were going bankrupt unless we could come up with a new business model.

Without the private equity firm that saw Time Out's global potential and invested in the company, we'd have become another casualty of the media revolution. Instead, we launched the free London magazine and grew our readership exponentially. We took the best of the old Time Out and tried to make it new again for a new generation.

It was an incredibly difficult transition. Some people will always love it the way it was before: like "Doctor Who", people love the Time Out of their era. I got death threats for cutting the TV section, and and we had several large layoffs, which put everyone on edge. But everyone always pulled together and overcame the pain. Time Out has always been more like a huge, dysfunctional family than the globe-spanning media corporation it has become.'

Caroline McGinn

London editor 2013-17 and global editor-in-chief since 2017

'Like most Londoners, I didn't come from London, and Time Out really was my best friend in the city when I arrived here. It gave me a sense of all of the things I was moving to the city for: the amazing cultural aspiration and the freedom to be who you wanted to be.

My time at Time Out has been a period of triumph, disaster and everything in between. Google, Facebook and the other internet giants have not only colonised the search of information – which was crucial to Time Out as a listings bible – but also eaten up ad revenue. But despite the media apocalypse, Time Out has flown from strength to strength.

Shifting to free distribution, first in London, then New York, Barcelona and other cities, has unleashed the most glorious kind of freedom. It's allowed us to find our soul again: to find out how we want to look and to say what we want to say. It's been massively liberating to be able to create covers that don't have to sell the magazine.

London – and the audience that we speak to and listen to here – has developed a strong collective sense of identity as a principled, progressive, diverse city. That's something I've really felt during the recurring crises of the last few years, from the riots of 2011 to the Grenfell Tower fire. There's also been incredible investment, democracy and pride in the cultural sector: we're still reaping the benefits of free entry at museums and galleries. From highbrow popular theatre to the rise of grime, we've seen urban culture across the spectrum draw on deep local roots and go global.

For Time Out, the city is always the star. All that any individual editor does is find a way for us to be a window on the London, the New York, the Madrid or the Melbourne of their particular era.'

The most ridiculous
...s we've overheard
...ew York this week

"I don't need a
...yfriend. I have
...shed potatoes."

"...le looks like a
...ppet, but I just
...an't decide
which one."

"...ting is so tough
... In the Midwest,
...uld clean up."

GRATIS BO...

Coordina Marta Salicrú
www.timeout.cat/concerts

Gaudeix de la ciutat per la cara

Metropolitain
Modelled after the Parisian Metro, hence the na...
Metropolitain's High Street stop transports din...
thanks to its industrial interior design and rela...
The menu features contemporary Gallic classic...
outstanding gratin dauphinoise, which is basic...
sliced potatoes and layers of cheese that are cut...
blocks. The beautiful presentation shows off th...
taste speaks for itself. Not for squares, $58. 46...
Sai Ying Pun, 6271 6102; french-creations.com

Atelier Vivanda
Located on Wan Chai's trendy Ship Stre...
looks and feels as if it's been imported fro...
well, it has. The chain originated in the F...
our city. It specialises in meat, bien sur, b...
much success and the casual bistro has a...
also shine, particularly the gratin dauphi...
cream, sporting a sublime buttery textur...
side is served in a cast iron dish and com...
Wan Chai, 2109 1768; ateliervivanda.co...

...d potato which have been sprinkled wi...
Elizabeth Purvis munches on our city...

YOUR SHANGHAI
CHECKLIST
Don't miss a beat with this
month's must-dos

← **Cynar J...**
When a mojit...
from college. ...
this delicious...
bartender Je...
Presented in...
filled with a...

Drinking
Edited by Elizabeth Atkinson
timeout.com/chicago/bars
@elizabethi

A Semana

...ed his languorous, yet
...rimey vocal style and
..., set on looped and
...undbeds of woozy,
...ychedelia, electronica and
... soul/blues. A member of
...ed new hip hop generation,
... Black Hippy, Odd Future
...sh Gambino, he appeals to
...hip hop heads and leftfield
...ike, and these shows are a
...Go see why the dude in the
...es Fuck Down' beanie is
...ch a stir. **Sharon O'Connell**

...allroom Tue June 5 and
...6 *Further listening:*
...rl.com/TOasap

Emirates Stadium Fri June...
June 2, Mon June 4
Further listening:
www.tinyurl.com/TOcoldplay

World-conquering stadium r...
I have a confession. I've see...
Coldplay twice in the past t...
months. This is a lot for a pe...
who doesn't own a single C...
album. Sure, there's still a p...
in my heart for the tender m...
of 'Don't Panic' and 'Shiver...
their more recent hits – feat...
reliably anthemic variations...
'Woah/Oh-oh/Woo' refrain...
sound quite as life-affirming...

Música
i nit

Londoners have their say

'LONDON
MUST B...

Sydney for
cheapskates

Zhang...
film fo...
separa...
lost sp...
agains...
→ Sund...

Arts &
Culture
Edited by Dee Jefferson
timeout.com/sydney

Modern

What's the craziest way you've tried to lose weight?

...ate a single
...nt of Ben and
...rry's a day
...even yogurt.

I put tobacco
on everything –
meal at 8am
even yogurt.

I ate one
meal at 8am
and one at

Sex &
Dating
Edited by Jillian Anthony
timeout.com/newyork/sex-dating

...d Day and The Apple Ca...

...ges for a one-day London
...nd then...
...we were a bit suspicious
...Apple Cart's *raison d'être.*
...arquees already in place
...Day, this second one-day
...ame organisers –
...bands with live comedy,
...interactive art – plus
...of: quick, fill those tents
...ver's about! Now we
...re's a clear
...hical demarcation.
...rned to this
...the magazine
...want Field Day.
...ed here via
...own, you'll want
...Cart. Or
...other

way – are you wearing a twee...
jacket? Yes = Field Day. Yes...
I can't get this baby up-chuck...
lapel = The Apple Cart.
   Field Day, now in its sixth y...
still the best way to binge on...
hyped indie-pop, time-honou...
rock and erudite dancefloor...
without pitching a tent. The A...
Cart, returning for a second t...
   Field Day with a wand...
   attention span...
   a log-in for Mu...
   Field Day pres...
   sharp popste...
   erdinand debut...
   material at their firs...
   in two years, plu...
   Star stirring...
   for th...

Ara i
aquí
...reu Gomila, Maria Junyent
...l Ricard Martín
...neout.cat/barcelona

The Undateables

'It's impossible to overstate the importance of Time Out to London's thriving counterculture; without its coverage, fringe venues would have died for lack of an audience. I stayed for 30 years because what I was doing felt necessary. It was endlessly exciting to work for a magazine that made such a difference to London's cultural life.'

Sarah Kent, Time Out visual arts editor 1976-2006

→
March 2010
Design
Banksy

A year earlier, Time Out had asked: 'Is the writing on the wall for Banksy?' Apparently not. The elusive Bristolian had a movie out, and designed Time Out's cover alongside an exclusive interview. Art director Nick Booth describes working via email with the anarchic artist as 'a voyage into an abyss', but adds, 'Banksy was very respectful – and in the end his cover was fucking brilliant.'

'Time Out: it's impossible that you are 50! You are eternally young, revealing all the unexpected pleasures and hidden corners of a city I was born in, and have lived in and loved in all my life. My life as a Londoner has been enriched by you.'

Dame Helen Mirren, actor

→
May 2012
Illustration
Matt Herring

'Peter Blake was originally supposed to design a cover for Queen Elizabeth's diamond jubilee,' explains art editor Anthony Huggins. 'He did it, but it wasn't quite right. So we sent his design to subscribers and commissioned illustrator Matt Herring to do this alternative, Sex Pistols-inspired version. It was a bit of a dry subject, so – in Time Out style – we wanted to do something that didn't take itself too seriously!'

Time Out

Lond

BY ROYAL APPOINTMENT... NOT
TIMEOUT.COM/LONDON
May 31 – June 6 2012

The Diamond JubiLee

Inside

Four days of fun, frolics and free street parties as London goes royally bonkers

Wham, bam, thank you ma'am!

Plus
Plan B: 'The kids will riot again'

£3.25
No.2180

9 771479 705062

01

02

03

04

→
**Time Out Barcelona,
March 2010**
Concept and design
Diego Piccininno
Photography
Cristina Reche

'Brutal' is how María José Gómez, Time Out Barcelona's editor-in-chief, describes this cover announcing Barcelona's top 15 meat dishes. 'Our art director Diego bought the 400g steak in one of the best butcher shops in the city's famous Boquería market. The idea was risky and we did have doubts... until we saw the result.'

01 **Time Out Barcelona,
May 2014**
Design
Diego Piccininno

02 **Time Out Barcelona,
March 2011**
Design
Diego Piccininno
Photography
Cristina Reche

03 **Time Out Barcelona,
March 2018**
Design
Diego Piccininno

04 **Time Out Barcelona,
November 2017**
Design
Diego Piccininno
Photography
Irene Fernández

Time Out
Barcelona

100% CARN

ESMOLA ELS ULLALS!

15 TEMPTACIONS PER A CARNÍVORS

LA GUIA DE RESTAURANTS DEFINITIVA PER
ASSABORIR ELS MILLORS PLATS DE VEDELLA,
XAI, BOU, LLETÓ, GARRÍ I CAÇA A BARCELONA

+ LOS PLANETAS
POP FLAMENC AL
FESTIVAL DE CAJÓN!

JAPAN WEEKEND
MANGA I VIDEOJOCS
AL PALAU SANT JORDI

GUANYA!
Entrades dobles
per als concerts
de Marc Parrot i de
Maria de Medeiros
TIMEOUT.CAT

WWW.TIMEOUT.CAT
11- 17 DE MARÇ 2010
N. 109

1,95€

00109
9 771888 385008

'For as long as as I can remember, Time Out has been an essential part of the cultural fabric of London, a goldmine of information and a barometer of taste.'

Adrian Wootton, chief executive of Film London and the British Film Commission

→
September 2012
Design
Adam Fulrath

By the early twenty-tens, Time Out was in financial trouble. After 44 years as a paid-for title, the radical decision was taken to make the London magazine available for free, with editor Tim Arthur nervously leading the charge. 'I was so incredibly proud to be the editor of Time Out, but my biggest fear was being the *last* editor,' he remembers. 'For the cover of the first free issue, I wanted something bold with the vague feel of a propaganda poster. Everyone worked round the clock for months, re-engineering the magazine to create something that people would love again – and it worked. Circulation went from 55,000 to 300,000 overnight.'

Time Out

London

INSIDE
Free art
Free films
Free music
Free theatre
Free comedy
Free Time Out

TAKE ME, I'M YOURS.

The **BEST** things to do in London.
This week. Every week.

SEP 25–OCT 1 2012   No. 2197   **TIMEOUT.COM/LONDON**

'From its inception, Time Out has recognised that without the arts, there is no London. It has chronicled, guided and inspired the city's art scene, ensuring art's life-changing powers are accessible to everyone.'

John Studzinski, chairman of Create

→
January 2014
Design
'Art Is...', 2014
Tracey Emin CBE RA

Major British artists who've taken over Time Out's cover include Gilbert and George, Grayson Perry, David Shrigley, the Chapman Brothers and Bob and Roberta Smith, as well as Banksy (p93). But Tracey Emin's exclusive cover and feature for the 2014 art special was particularly exciting: the artist had given her first ever press interview in 1995 to Time Out art critic Sarah Kent.

'It's great Time Out is still going strong – it is the best way to find out what's happening in London.'

Katharine Hamnett, fashion designer

→
February 2014
Design
Adam Fulrath

'One classic Time Out trick is turning the cover into an iconic object,' says creative director Adam Fulrath. This image played on the ubiquitous yellow bags of famous department store Selfridges, revealing the shop as the top entry in the cover feature. 'It was easy to recreate the Selfridges font,' adds Fulrath, 'because Time Out and Selfridges share Franklin Gothic as a typeface.'

Time Out
London

MARY 11 – 17 2014 No. 2264
OUT.COM/LONDON

LONDON'S BEST SHOPS

What's number one? It's in the bag…

01

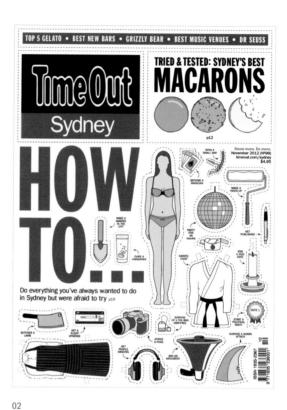

02

→

**Time Out Sydney,
November 2011**
Design
Tom Hislop

The lead feature in this Sydney
issue focused on vintage shops,
a theme picked up by designer
Tom Hislop: 'I decided to create
a homage to Andy Warhol's Brillo
boxes that commented on the
growing culture of consumerism,
using simple graphic
elements repetitively.'

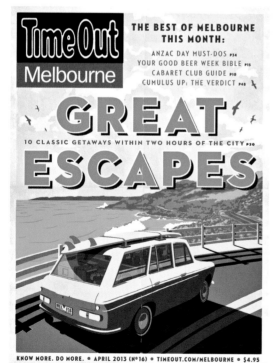

03

04

01 **Time Out Melbourne,
June 2013**
Illustration
Tom Hislop

02 **Time Out Sydney,
November 2012**
Illustration
Ashleigh Bowring

03 **Time Out Melbourne,
April 2013**
Illustration
Tom Hislop

04 **Time Out Sydney,
May 2017**
Illustration
*Reko Rennie,
'As the Crow Flies'*

NOVEMBER 2011 NO.87

$4.95

TimeOut
Sydney

Inside:
Sydney's hottest Thai restaurants p18

New!

Sydney's best
Shops ®

Antiques, hobbies, kitsch, bric-a-brac & more!

Great for Xmas!

Sydney's best fish & chips p88

BANKSY IN TOWN
Street artists come to Cockatoo Island for Outpost Project
p44

THEATRE SPECIAL
With guest writers Brendan Cowell, Kate Ritchie, Toby Schmitz & more
p72

SYDNEY'S BEST BAR
Winner announced!
p16

ISSN 1835-2367

9 771835 236001

11

NET WT. 3²/₃ OZ (160g). MADE IN SYDNEY, AUSTRALIA.

KNOW MORE. DO MORE. TIMEOUT.COM/SYDNEY

→
Time Out Tokyo, April 2014
Art director
Steve Nakamura
Photography
Takeshi Hanzawa
Styling
Kumiko Iijima
Hair and make-up
Masayoshi Okudaira

Time Out Tokyo has covered the
Japanese capital since 2009,
with Steve Nakamura art directing
every cover of the English-
language magazine since issue
two. He was also creative director
for its cover star, Japanese pop
icon Kyary Pamyu Pamyu. 'When
people think of Tokyo, what
generally comes to mind is food
and pop culture,' he explains. 'The
challenge here was to merge both
those elements.'

Time Out
Tokyo

APR - JUN 2014 NO.2
TIMEOUT.COM/TOKYO

WIN!
An elegant dinner for two, p40

INSIDE!
Japanese Food 101
The best beers, bars and hangover cures

Hanami hunt
Behold the cherry blossoms!

EAT LIKE A
TOKYOITE
Kyary Pamyu Pamyu kicks off our food odyssey

FREE

01

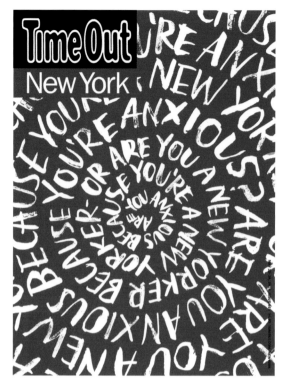

02

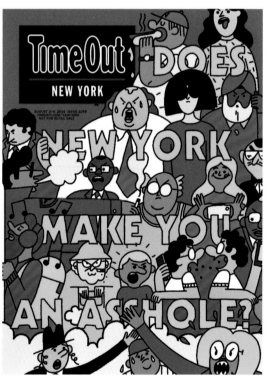

03

04

→
Time Out New York, June 2016
Design
Ashleigh Bowring

How do you visually represent
something as abstract as
revealing a city's secrets?
By literally hiding the coverline,
says global creative director Tom
Hislop. 'We were inspired by the
work of MC Escher, Magic Eye
books and other optical illusions.
Illustrating the cover was a
painstakingly manual process
that caused US art director
Ashleigh Bowring to go cross-
eyed. But it was worth it!'

01 **Time Out New York,
    September 2014**
    Photography
    Stephen Meierding

02 **Time Out New York,
    May 2014**
    Illustration
    Angela Southern

03 **Time Out New York,
    August 2016**
    Illustration
    Leon Edler

04 **Time Out New York,
    January 2018**
    Photography
    Stephen Meierding

Time Out
NEW YORK

JUNE 8–14, 2016 ISSUE 1052
TIMEOUT.COM/NEWYORK
NOT FOR RETAIL SALE

→
July 2016
Art director
Mark Neil
Text
Alexi Duggins

In the UK's 2016 EU referendum, the majority voted to leave – but in London, the vote went the other way. 'The referendum left the Time Out London team shaken and stunned,' says group CEO Julio Bruno. 'Our editor-in-chief asked me if I could meet the editorial team, and I reminded them of who we are: that Time Out is inclusive, diverse and an ambassador of the cities we serve. This award-winning cover was born after that get-together. It is a heartfelt personal letter from Time Out to the world about inclusion and diversity – values this city and Time Out have always stood for.'

'Time Out *is* London. Ours is a true world city. It's international, open, creative – values also embodied by Time Out through great writing, insights and a distinctive London sense of humour.'

Justine Simons, deputy mayor for culture and the creative industries

Dear World,

It's been quite a week here in London. But there's one thing we would like to make clear right now: people who were not born in this city are welcome here. Not just Europeans, everyone – no matter what nationality, race, creed, colour or shoe size.

Ask most Londoners what we love about this city and we'll say one thing: its diversity.

There is no place in this city for anyone who wants to make anyone else feel unwelcome. If you have a problem with people who look or sound different to you, you're not a real Londoner.

Our city has not changed. It remains a place that cherishes human beings of all nationalities and ethnic backgrounds. So, people of Europe and people of the world, thank you for making our city your home. No, let's rephrase that. Thank you for making YOUR city your home.

Yours, as always

Time At London

01

→
Time Out Lisbon,
September 2016
Design
João Caetano

A collective design effort by the Time Out Lisbon team resulted in this simple but striking visual concept, coordinated by art director João Caetano. Lisbon's official animal symbol – a crow – is engulfed in the colours of the rainbow flag, proclaiming the city's thriving LGBT+ scene and Time Out's celebration of sexual freedom across the globe.

02

03

04

01   **Time Out Lisbon,**
     July 2013
     Photography
     Hugo Neves

02   **Time Out Lisbon,**
     January 2014
     Photography
     Gonçalo F Santos

03   **Time Out Lisbon,**
     June 2012
     Photography
     Gonçalo F Santos

04   **Time Out Lisbon,**
     May 2017
     Photography
     Manuel Manso

14 A 20 DE SETEMBRO DE 2016 Nº 468 2,20€ (CONTINENTE)

LISBOA

**O QUE COMPRAR
E VESTIR NA
FASHION'S
NIGHT OUT**

**OS MELHORES
ÉCLAIRS DO PORTO
CHEGARAM
A LISBOA**

**SUPERNOVA:
A RECEPÇÃO AO
CALOIRO A QUE
QUEREMOS IR**

LISBOA
GAY

**NO ARRANQUE
DE MAIS UM QUEER LISBOA,
TRAÇAMOS O ROTEIRO
DOS ESPAÇOS LGBT
DE QUE MAIS GOSTAMOS.
DAS FESTAS AOS BARES,
DA MODA AO DESPORTO,
LISBOA ESTÁ CADA VEZ
MAIS FRIENDLY**

'Quite simply,
Time Out is London.
It travels with us to
work every Tuesday
morning and keeps
us company on
the way out for the
evening. It's a much
loved one-stop
shop to find out the
latest goings on in
our great city.'

Sharon Ament, director of the
Museum of London

→
October 2016
Illustration
Justin Metz

The Victorian print 'All Is Vanity' by
Charles Allan Gilbert inspired the
cover of this Halloween issue. Art
editor Mark Neil commissioned
Photoshop illustrator Justin Metz
to create a skull emerging out of
a dark, cloudy London sky: 'The
image needed to spookily appear
out of a real-life setting. Of all
the famous London landmarks,
Big Ben's clock tower and face
worked the best – it gave it a great
gothic vibe.'

TimeOut
LONDON

London's dark side

→
**Time Out Chicago,
December 2016**
*Photography
Stephen Meierding
Styling
Maya Evans Judd*

Showcasing the global diversity
of Chicago's food scene with
a simple, dynamic image
was the aim here, says global
creative director Tom Hislop.
'The thing that resonates with
me from this cover is the power
of a good idea. But what was
really interesting to see was the
appropriation of the concept from
competitors afterwards!'

01

02

01 **Time Out San Francisco,
October 2017**
*Illustration
Tom Hislop*

02 **Time Out Los Angeles,
April 2018**
*Paper art
Owen Gildersleeve*

03 **Time Out Los Angeles,
July 2017**
*Illustration
Tom Hislop*

04 **Time Out Miami,
May 2017**
*Creative director
Tom Hislop*

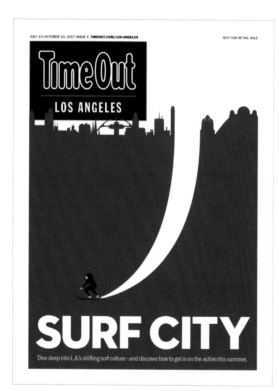

03

04

TimeOut
CHICAGO

Gulp!

We're ready to dig
into this year's 100 best
dishes and drinks.

DECEMBER 2016–FEBRUARY 2017
ISSUE 6 TIMEOUT.COM/CHICAGO
NOT FOR RETAIL SALE

→
**Time Out Tel Aviv,
February 2017**
*Photography
Netta Dror
Art director
Leor Gal*

Time Out Tel Aviv aims to reflect
the voice of its politicised readers.
'Our audience allows us to be
outrageous and underground
without the need for touristy
vibes,' says editor-in-chief Nof
Nathansohn. The 2017 sex issue's
coverline is a pun on the Hebrew
words for 'discussion' and 'bush'
– 'it could be loosely translated
as "pub(l)ic hair", explains
Nathansohn – and bar a few
concerned parents, Tel Avivians
adored this provocative portrayal
of femininity.

Time Out
תל אביב

השיח
הציבורי

סקס והעיר: איך התל אביבים
עושים את זה? אנחנו
שאלנו, אתם עניתם

→
Time Out Beijing, January 2018
Design
Patrick Joseph Moore and
Wang Qian
Photography
Chen Chao

A simple idea – harnessing and
subverting the art jargon of a
gallery caption – turns the cover of
Time Out Beijing into a conceptual
artwork in itself. Launched in
2003, Time Out China publishes
English-language magazines in
both the capital and the cultural
hub of Shanghai.

FREE
NO. 159
Jan-Feb 2018
CN42-1750/GO

新旅行 英文版

Voyage

www.timeoutbeijing.com

ISSN 1674-5116

The museum issue, 2018

Time Out Beijing (b. 2004)
Digital ink print on paper, 20.6 x 27.3cm

In this seminal work, lifestyle artist T. O.
Beijing continues their exploration of the
urban environment, stimulating heightened
interaction between museums and the self.

Through engaging interplay of visual and
textual elements, the piece invites the viewer
into enriching realms filled with ancient
artefacts, marvellous machines, scientific
endeavour, heartbreak and watermelons.

'I can remember Tony Elliott coming in to my Fulham Road Clothes Shop in 1968 with Time Out as a Xeroxed sheet. Look what this humble beginning has now become! The amazing flowering of a vision!'

Dame Zandra Rhodes, fashion designer

→
Time Out Hong Kong, April 2018
Design
Phoebe Cheng

'Freedom', 'nightlife', 'convenience' and 'dim sum' are among the mass of sticky notes giving a taste of '50 reasons why we love Hong Kong'. Phoebe Cheng, creative director, enlisted colleagues to write the notes for this collage cover that launched the Traditional Chinese edition of Time Out Hong Kong.

2018年4月-6月　No. 001　TIMEOUT.COM/HONG-KONG/HK

TimeOut
香港

靚女！

人情味

動感之都

這裏是我家

大都市

自由

夜生活

雲吞麵

24小時

都有野食

西貢

好方便

郊遊

地鐵

行山

衛市

點心

夜景

李氏力牆

廣東歌

美食天堂

多元文化

四通八達

銅鑼灣

安定

夜夜笙歌

茶餐廳

精彩日與夜

個我們愛上
香港的原因

'Whatever you're into, you can find it in our amazing city. For the last 50 years, Time Out has been the place to go to find out what's on. It started with London and is now the go-to guide for cities right across the world. Here's to the next 50 years!'

Sadiq Khan, Mayor of London

→
August 2017
Illustration
Tom Havell
Text
Chris Waywell and Gail Tolley

In recent years, the cover star of Time Out London has increasingly been the city itself. 'When we thought about it, an awful lot of the capital was green,' says editor Gail Tolley. With ideas contributed by the editorial team, the only-in-London 'swatches' on the colour chart are a portrait of the city painted in just one colour.

TimeOut
LONDON

Regrettable Whatsapp sext
C25 M00 Y37 K00

Palm Vaults
C44 M00 Y42 K00

Festival Hall roof
C32 M00 Y27 K00

Pie 'n' mash liquor
C31 M06 Y59 K02

Half-eaten Wasabi
C25 M00 Y50 K00

Hipster succulent
C54 M09 Y49 K04

Bethnal
C79 M01 Y99 K05

Old Camden punk mohawk
C47 M00 Y99 K00

Matcha gelato
C43 M00 Y55 K00

Uber vomiter
C25 M00 Y80 K00

Trafalgar Square Yoda
C25 M09 Y48 K02

Smacked cucumber
C30 M00 Y52 K00

Cabbies' shelter
C94 M00 Y80 K00

Francis Drake Bowls Club
C85 M00 Y99 K00

Wimbledon (Day one)
C65 M00 Y99 K00

Brisbane Road
C55 M00 Y74 K00

Avo on toast
C26 M03 Y75 K00

Wimbledon (Finals)
C20 M00 Y68 K00

Kale smoothie
C99 M03 Y99 K16

District line
C99 M02 Y95 K12

Veggie Pret
C87 M00 Y99 K00

Waitrose bagging area
C66 M00 Y99 K01

Golders
C50 M00 Y75X K00

Kingston parakeet
C22 M00 Y87 K08

Tooting terrapin
C72 M13 Y99 K39

London Irish
C99 M04 Y67 K20

Begging Bowl rabbit curry
C42 M15 Y80 K09

Citymapper
C90 M00 Y99 K00

'Wicked'
C63 M00 Y98 K00

The Churchill Arms
C61 M00 Y80 K00

Harrods doorman
C59 M11 Y99 K58

Discarded Christmas tree
C80 M09 Y86 K38

Commons backbench
C76 M17 Y69 K35

Canal scum
C45 M06 Y99 K32

Ramesh, the ZSL iguana
C72 M00 Y61 K00

Mushy peas
C76 M07 Y99 K00

Professor
C93 M20 Y99 K55

Those new fag packets
C44 M19 Y84 K61

Occasional Routemaster
C99 M09 Y98 K45

Ambassadors' curtains
C75 M00 Y99 K30

47 percent of our city
C99 M00 Y99 K00

The Green Issue

Afterword

Julio Bruno

CEO of Time Out Group

'It all began in London in 1968, when Tony Elliott created Time Out to help people explore the exciting things that were happening all over the city. Fifty years on, this is still at the heart of everything we do. We continue to inspire and enable people to make the most of the city – only today we are present in 108 cities in 39 countries, reaching a global monthly audience of 217 million.

Over the years, the brand has maintained its status as the go-to source of inspiration for locals and visitors alike, making Time Out the only true global marketplace for city life. Our unique, curated content about the best things to do in cities – written by professional journalists – has a huge influence on the travel and leisure purchasing decisions of hundreds of millions of people around the world. While we still write about the best city experiences, we now also create and deliver them.

Every year, millions of customers book theatre tickets and hotels, buy exclusive offers or book restaurants with us. Or they visit Time Out Market, which opened in 2014 in Lisbon. This is the world's first food and cultural market, bringing the best of the city together under one roof based on editorial curation. With 3.6 million visitors in 2017, it is Portugal's most popular attraction. It is such a success story that we are opening new Time Out Markets in Miami, New York, Boston, Chicago and Montreal, and we continue to scope sites in other great cities around the world.

As a regular traveller, I have always been a huge fan of Time Out: my best friend in the cities I love and the cities I couldn't wait to explore. So leading the future of this iconic brand is a personal milestone that means a lot to me.

Every single one of us at Time Out is immensely proud that our content remains as relevant now as when we first started. I like to say that we are in the happiness business, because Time Out exists to make sure people have fun and enjoy life in the world's most exciting cities.'

→
Julio Bruno (front and centre)
with the Time Out London team,
July 2018

Acknowledgements

Putting this book together wouldn't have been even remotely feasible without the incredibly hard work of Time Out supermen Tom Hislop and Ben Rowe, as well as the caption-writing chops of Tristan Parker, Sonya Barber (once a Time Outer, always a Time Outer), Laura Lee Davies, Megan Carnegie, Rose Johnstone, Chris Waywell and Liz Tray.

Thanks also to Eleanor Scott at Somerset House for letting me adapt her excellent Tony Elliott interview; to Julio Bruno and Alex Rieck for the Afterword; to Dan Collins and David Woodley for their long memories; to Kiran Chopra and Anne Crompton for legal advice; to MJ Gómez, JP Oliveira, Kenneth Tan, Nof Nathansohn, Mao Kawakami and all the art directors across the globe for help with international covers; to Rasendu Shah and Helen McFarland for retouching and picture assistance; to Esther Jackson and Anne Gerrish for raiding the archives; and to Caroline McGinn, Christine Petersen, Séverine Philardeau and of course the entire team at Unicorn Publishing Group for making this project possible in the first place.

Special thanks to all of the former and current staff who answered questions about their time at Time Out, especially Pearce Marchbank and all the former editors for their detailed and occasionally lurid insights. Thanks to all the illustrious Londoners and their teams for their Time Out memories and words of congratulation; to the artists, photographers, illustrators and designers who allowed us to showcase their work from across the decades; and above all to Tony, whose big idea has made the last 50 years of city life much more exciting. ■ *James Manning*

www.timeout.com/50